DILIGENCE

Also by Dzigar Kongtrul

DILIGENCE

The JOYFUL ENDEAVOR
of the BUDDHIST PATH

Dzigar Kongtrul
Edited by Jennifer Shippee

FOREWORD BY PEMA CHÖDRÖN

SHAMBHALA

Shambhala Publications, Inc.
2129 13th Street
Boulder, Colorado 80302
www.shambhala.com

© 2024 by Mangala Shri Bhuti

The translation of the verses of the Diligence Chapter, from
The Way of the Bodhisattva (Boulder: Shambhala, 2006), is used
with permission of the Padmakara Translation Group.

Cover art: Demogorgona/Shutterstock
Cover design: Daniel Urban-Brown
Interior design: Kate Huber-Parker

9 8 7 6 5 4 3 2 1

First Edition
Printed in the United States of America

Shambhala Publications makes every effort
to print on acid-free, recycled paper.
Shambhala Publications is distributed worldwide by
Penguin Random House, Inc., and its subsidiaries.

Library of Congress Cataloging-in-Publication Data
Names: Kongtrul, Dzigar, author. | Shippee, Jennifer, editor.
Title: Diligence: the joyful endeavor of the Buddhist path/Dzigar Kongtrul;
edited by Jennifer Shippee.
Description: Boulder: Shambhala Publications, 2024.
Identifiers: LCCN 2023057972 | ISBN 9781645472360 (trade paperback)
Subjects: LCSH: Diligence—Religious aspects—Buddhism. | Virtues. | Buddhism—
Doctrines.
Classification: LCC BQ4570.D55 K66 2024
LC record available at https://lccn.loc.gov/2023057972

CONTENTS

FOREWORD BY

PEMA CHÖDRÖN

When we think of the Buddhist path, diligence might not be the first thing that comes to mind. Most of us associate compassion, peace, meditation, or perhaps metaphysical teachings on the nature of phenomena with the Buddha and his wisdom. Nonetheless, diligence—or enthusiasm, as it is also sometimes translated from the Tibetan term *tsöndrü*—sits there in the middle of the six *paramitas*, or perfections: the core practices of aspiring buddhas or bodhisattvas. The word *diligence* might sound stern, or make us feel uneasy, until we get curious and start to explore its essential meaning as the fourth paramita.

The paramita of diligence works like a miracle ingredient, bringing eagerness to all we do. On the bodhisattva path, our eagerness is guided by wisdom, and what we are committing to on that path is anything but trivial. Without the paramita of eagerness or enthusiasm, we might push too hard or give up altogether. The key is to find a balance between "not too tight" and "not too loose," not too zealous and not too laid back. As Zen Master Suzuki Roshi said, "What we are doing here is so important we had better not take it too seriously!"

My root teacher, the late Chögyam Trungpa Rinpoche, encouraged us to lead our lives as an experiment—a suggestion that has been very important to me. Approaching all we encounter in life as an experiment encourages us to try things this way and that, because either way we have nothing to lose. I first learned this liberating flexibility from

Trungpa Rinpoche but also see it embodied in my second teacher, Dzigar Kongtrul Rinpoche. Both of these masters radiate tremendous energy and enthusiasm for every endeavor in which they engage. This has allowed them to accomplish an amazing amount in their lives.

Dzigar Kongtrul Rinpoche relates to his students, to all his various activities, and to his path itself with a relentless force of goodness and joy, of vigor and stamina—in a word, enthusiasm. Where does that seemingly ceaseless strength and endurance come from? What is its source?

It seems the trick is not to become caught up in hope and fear. We can put our whole heart into anything we do, but if we let our attitude freeze into a stance of for or against, we're setting ourselves up for stress. Instead, we could just proceed with curiosity, being open to where this experiment may lead. This kind of inquisitiveness captures the spirit of enthusiasm and keeps each moment fresh, alive, and joyful.

Wind is a good metaphor for diligence. Like the wind in the sails of a ship, there's nothing heavy-handed about it. It doesn't take thousands of people to push a ship across the ocean; when the sails go up, the wind easily moves the vessel forward.

Once we have trust in the teachings, we'll naturally take delight in virtue. When I realized, for example, that Shantideva's instructions could cut through my unhappiness, I became enthusiastic about applying them. In such cases, taking delight in virtue means working wisely with my emotions and learning to gently tame my mind. It means reaching out to offer kindness and support to as many beings as possible—and doing this eagerly, not out of a sense of duty.

I can tell you from experience that when there's a shift toward eagerness, life takes on a whole new meaning—not the meaning that comes from careers or relationships but the meaning that arises from using anything and everything that happens as an opportunity to wake up.

Dzigar Kongtrul Rinpoche's book on Shantideva's Diligence Chapter is about greeting whatever we meet in our everyday lives with joy and eagerness. Rinpoche shows us how we can transform whatever we encounter in life into an opportunity to rise above, to shed our indifference, and to take hold of our deepest potential. There will always be challenges, but they need not be seen as obstacles. With the tools of diligence, everything can become part of the path to enlightenment.

PREFACE

May this Diligence Chapter and the commentary on the practice of tsöndru bring insight into the various hindrances that we may or may not be aware of, and may we thus overcome all obstacles and manifest our greatest potential—that of becoming a bodhisattva in this modern world. A bodhisattva is defined by *bodhichitta*. Bodhichitta, in essence, is a warm heart that feels care and concern for all living beings and joyfully endeavors to liberate them from both the immediate and long-term suffering of samsara. It is the wish to selflessly guide and deliver beings to their own enlightenment, which is their true nature, potential, and birthright.

May the merit of this book bring immense benefit to the world. May I remain a humble, simple practitioner of this noble lineage. If anything written here sounds arrogant, or as if I know it all, I confess to the reader that this is not a strength of mine but a flaw, and I therefore ask your forgiveness. My intention is merely to exaggerate some points of our common neuroses in order to illustrate a clear picture of what we all need to work on.

INTRODUCTION

ACCOMPLISHING OUR ASPIRATIONS

We all have aspirations in life. We have dreams, work hard to better ourselves, and seek to make our lives meaningful. We apply ourselves in many areas and wrestle to discern what brings lasting fulfillment, joy, and peace—beyond just the fleeting moments of these experiences.

Despite our aspirations and efforts, many of us often feel that something is holding us back, particularly where it is most meaningful and personally fulfilling. Sometimes it is an outer impediment or something that we can't control—an external force or person that prevents us from achieving our goals. Much of the time, however, the impediment is not outside, but has more to do with ourselves. Something internal prevents us from doing what it takes to make progress in fulfilling our deepest wishes and aspirations.

That internal thing can have many faces and manifest in various ways. The Buddha's teachings collectively define these inner impediments as "laziness." We might think, *I am not lazy. I get up early, go to the gym, get my kids to school on time, go to work, make dinner, clean the house, call my parents, and volunteer my service to the community on the weekends.* The kind of laziness that the Buddhist teachings address, however, is most likely not what comes to mind when we first hear the word *laziness.*

1

In the context of learning about diligence and how to identify and adopt what supports us in achieving our goals, *laziness* is defined as whatever prevents or hinders us from getting to what we really want to do. In the Diligence Chapter of *The Way of the Bodhisattva* (*Bodhicharyavatara*), the eighth-century Buddhist master Shantideva addresses this laziness. Shantideva lays bare our internal habits of procrastination, preoccupations, and distractions with which we tend to fill the gaps in our days—the things that we know are a waste of time or an avoidance of getting to what is most meaningful, but that we do anyway. In this context, laziness is not caused by outer conditions; laziness is about us—about how we unconsciously, and sometimes consciously, prevent ourselves from progressing in the way we wish.

Shantideva's book, as a whole, is a profound exposition on the six *paramitas*, or transcendent perfections—generosity, moral discipline, patience, diligence, meditation, and wisdom. Collectively, these are the practices of a *bodhisattva*, or an aspiring bodhisattva—someone who has committed to the path of awakening for the benefit of all beings. It is said, over and over, that the paramita of diligence is needed in order to progress on the path of the other five paramitas: those with diligence will advance swiftly, while those without it will not.

In this book, we will explore the seventy-six verses that comprise Shantideva's Diligence Chapter. They will be presented in the same order as in *The Way of the Bodhisattva* and discussed thematically; as a result, sometimes a span of verses will be introduced in one chapter of this book, and the individual verses will appear throughout subsequent chapters.

Diligence is a tool that not only helps us progress in the paramitas, it also assists us in understanding what laziness is, how it manifests in our mind stream, and how we can identify and work with unconscious habits that undermine our efforts and stagnate our progress. Diligence helps us on our path of the Dharma and supports us to be more productive in other areas of our life—spiritual or worldly. Diligence, therefore, allows us to fulfill our deepest aspirations in all fields of interest.

Diligence—*tsöndru* in Tibetan, and *virya* in Sanskrit—in essence, is learning to find joy in what we are working on or engaged with. The practice of diligence utilizes enjoyment and delight as means to sustain ourselves and accomplish our goals. After all, if there is no delight in what we are doing, how can we continue to work hard and apply ourselves in that effort?

So what is this joy and how do we find it? How do we cultivate it, sustain it, and make it our own? When we do happen to enjoy what we are doing, it can almost seem to be by chance, especially when we are tasked with things we feel obligated or pressured to do. In the context of this book, we are mainly speaking about the spiritual path and how to cultivate authentic joy in that realm. But joyful exertion—as tsöndru can also be translated—can apply to any and every area of our lives, whether spiritual or conventional, ordinary or extraordinary.

We have all experienced being tired and totally exhausted while still inspired to carry on with what we are doing. If we love what we are doing, even if it is hard work and we are exhausted, we can remain buoyant, resilient, and energized in our mind and body. In these cases, we are usually cognizant of a larger accomplishment we are aiming to achieve, and working toward that greater goal gives us joy, even when we are flagging. That joy and energy show us the power of perspective. Thinking intellectually about a broader perspective, however, is not enough to sustain us for the long haul, particularly on the spiritual path. The spiritual path of liberation is not a short-term goal—we are in it for the endgame, so to speak, and the details matter. How we relate to the moment-to-moment-ness of what we are doing while maintaining a long-term vision, particularly on the spiritual path, is critical to seeing it through to the end.

How do we cultivate this larger perspective and also keep our joy in the details? There are many cases in which we already do this. In a conventional work setting, for instance, when we are motivated and work hard, we are usually thinking about what we will gain from our efforts—we have an image of that in our mind. The anticipated future gain inspires us. People work hard for their salary at the end of the month so that they can take their sweetheart out to a nice dinner or buy a gift for a loved one, pay the mortgage, get a reliable car, send their children to school, find good health insurance, or make the payments on the loans for these things. People often hope for a promotion or a bonus and do extra work at home or after hours in order to secure that. We know that if we don't demonstrate a sense of loyalty and commitment at work, we won't be valued and won't get the reward we are striving so hard for. This motivates us—the prospect of a potential future gain and the potential future loss of that gain.

Effectively pursuing the details of our job on a day-to-day basis makes it possible to capture that potential future gain. Thinking we can come to work at any time, complete our tasks or not, play computer games, or scroll on our phones—we know that if we act this way we will lose our job, and thus the income that brings certain freedoms and pleasures. So we learn to engage in and enjoy our life at work as we become integrated with what we must do. Our attention to the details of our job, whatever it may be, lends us integrity and brings satisfaction. We meet the details of our daily tasks with that integrity, and also look forward to achieving the gain we want in the end.

In this, it's not so much the salary or the funds that we hold as the motivating image in our mind—although for some that can indeed be the goal. For most people, it is what they can and want to do with the spending power that they gain through employment that forms the impetus. And for this end, many will make great efforts. In Japan and many other countries, people work from 7 a.m. to 9 p.m., six or even seven days a week—and they also do extra work in order to show their commitment to a company. Some people, including Elon Musk, are known to sleep in their offices or cubicles, on a cot or under their desks, because they have no time to go home. This is how they make their way up the ladder, eventually becoming the boss or CEO of their company, finally able to flash their company card and watch as people admire their status and buying power.

These examples of worldly efforts are meant to show us that we are naturally capable of great diligence. Diligence is not foreign or esoteric, nor is it difficult to apply, particularly when we know what we want to gain or achieve.

On the spiritual path, we also consider the future gain from applying ourselves, as well as what we may lose by being lazy and neglecting the details of our path. Just as in the working world, it is not only about advancing to a certain level for its own sake. Just as our paycheck gives us the freedom to live and do the things we wish to do, the gains on our spiritual path also bring us freedom—freedom from being buried under our destructive, habitual, reactive patterns and from the blind self-importance that drives us helplessly to react in ways that grind us down, causing ourselves and others great suffering. The gain is discovering our inherently resilient heart and our basic goodness, which is naturally infused with loving kindness, compassion, and joy toward all living beings. The gain is learning the joy and benefit of virtuous practices such as generosity, moral discipline, and patience, which in turn make us more buoyant and resilient amid the ocean of suffering of *samsara*—the indefinite wandering through birth, misery, death, and rebirth. The gain is studying our relative and absolute nature and acquiring the knowledge of emptiness and selflessness, which releases us from our ignorance and obscurations. The gain is becoming liberated, which in turn frees us to be of benefit to others. All these gains make us available to help others. The prospect of attaining these gains is greatly influenced by the perspective we hold in our mind, and our perspective is brought to life by the details of the path and our day-to-day, moment-to-moment experiences.

Similarly, the prospect of loss due to not engaging—or engaging, but with misunderstanding or in an improper way—can also motivate us. Here we contemplate the potential risks of not following through. If we do not at least aspire to relate to a genuine spiritual practice and path, we can easily be swallowed up by our ignorance, our self-absorption, and our (possibly misguided) projections of the world and others. These things can bring us great suffering and confusion and can make us act out in all kinds of unintended ways. It doesn't stop there, however, because once we do or say something hurtful to another, we must also experience the consequences of our actions in this life and the next. So we want to learn to motivate ourselves and take delight in engaging in virtuous actions, speech, and mindsets that bring benefit to ourselves and others.

Diligence, tsöndru, or joyful exertion is the delighted and inspired desire to engage in the way of the bodhisattva. The bodhisattva on the path works to see themselves and all others as absolutely equal in wishing for happiness and freedom from suffering, strives to exchange themself for others, and finally learns to cherish others even more than themself. The way of the bodhisattva is to learn how to joyfully practice all of this based on the Buddha's wisdom and skillful means.

THE THREE KINDS OF LAZINESS: A SNAPSHOT

Given how inspiring and wonderful this is, why do we often struggle to stay on course and complete what we know to be positive and good? Why do we give up or not follow through? What is it that happens along the way? The short answer is, we are lazy. And this is not just the lie around and do nothing kind of lazy, although that is one type of laziness. Our laziness is cleverer than that. It uses endless, self-justifying distractions and even self-denigration to disguise itself, ultimately preventing us from getting to what we truly wish to do with our precious time and life.

The Buddha's teachings define three categories of laziness. Whenever we try to fully engage the path—or anything really—these three kinds of laziness can creep in and block us from accomplishing what we set out to do. Identifying our laziness is the first step in learning the practice of diligence or joyful exertion.

The first type of laziness is perhaps the one we are most familiar with when we think about *being lazy*. Sometimes we can feel so heavy and lethargic—emotionally, mentally, and physically—it is like living with a carb crash. When we give in to that feeling, the fatigue then takes over our whole being. This can be a place we tend to fall into. It is like turning over in bed and staying under the covers. More than just that, we feel deeply attached to staying there. This type of laziness is not about getting genuine rest and rejuvenation. It is a hideout, a cop-out, a way of procrastinating or avoiding what we want to do—mainly due to our attachment to our fatigue, or the excuse that our fatigue gives us, and then slumping into that as an escape.

Second, there is the laziness of being distracted by mundane, fruitless activities, like the numbing "pleasure" of scrolling through Instagram, following endless news cycles, or fussing around the house, monotonously doing this and that, or any other activity that we instinctually know to be procrastination. This second kind of laziness keeps us from getting to our task—what we want to do or what is most meaningful and fulfilling—particularly given the limited amount of time we usually have to spare.

The third kind of laziness is basically giving up before we even try. This laziness is a form of self-denigration or low self-esteem. We think, *I can't; there is no way. I am not worthy. I am not capable. Others are different, maybe, but I cannot do this.* This is laziness disguised as low self-esteem, and it can run deep and be quite subtle. This form of laziness keeps us in our comfortable habitual cocoon, where we feel "safe" as we repeatedly tell ourselves that we are unable to do this or that. We can trap ourselves in this place by selecting scenarios or calling up memories that confirm for us how unworthy or incapable we are, so we might as well not bother trying.

Shantideva explores these three categories of laziness in depth, stripping back the layers of each to expose what is really happening and what is driving our behavior. After making us more self-aware of these tendencies, he introduces ways to think and talk to ourselves honestly one-on-one. He gives us powerful tools to help us navigate the murky waters of laziness, specifically—as we will learn over the course of this book—the four allies and the two strengths, which we can employ in addition to our own self-reflective awareness.

Shantideva lived in eighth-century India and grew up as a prince before turning fully toward the Dharma. How he unravels and reveals the workings of the mind shows us, remarkably, that we have not changed much over the centuries—either in terms of our basic neuroses or, thankfully, in terms of our basic strengths. What worked then still works now. As people struggled with their minds then, we still struggle in more or less the same way now. Shantideva shows us, however, that we are not as stuck as we may think or assume or feel—unless, of course, we insist on holding on to our self-importance and staying in our familiar cocoon.

Exploring feelings of unworthiness and other expressions of low self-esteem from this perspective can open us to other ways of relating to this pervasive modern-day experience. Understanding how low self-esteem can disguise itself as laziness can also lighten our feelings around how we see ourselves. Maybe we are not the lowest of the low . . . maybe we are just a little bit lazy! Maybe seeing our time wasted in scrolling on our phones, for instance, not as a heavy-handed form of addiction, but simply as another facet of laziness could bring some space into our minds, allowing us to chuckle at ourselves or sigh with good-natured laughter. That spaciousness and tender perspective toward ourselves can help us let go, put down our device, and joyfully turn to something more meaningful and fulfilling.

And maybe when we want to pull the covers over our head, desperately holding out for a few more minutes of sleep—even when we know we will only be tossing and turning—we can, again with a touch of tender humor toward ourselves, see that temptation as a tricky seduction of laziness. Knowing this, we can then simply take a deep breath, let go, and joyfully sit up and relate to our mind more directly.

It is liberating to see our laziness for what it is. Rather than being controlled by it, honestly noticing our tendencies to deny, avoid, and procrastinate can help us reflect and ask ourselves, *What am I doing? What do I really want to do?* Honest self-reflection creates space in our mind—room to see what is happening, and then some space, for instance, to apply one of the four allies or two strengths, thus shifting our mind, and with it our perspective.

The essence of diligence is joy. Finding genuine joy means personally connecting with what we are doing. Approaching what is most meaningful in our lives with a strict must-do attitude does not bring much joy, nor is it sustainable. A heavy-handed approach usually makes us procrastinate and avoid things even more. We want to explore why we find some things meaningful. We want to understand how they fulfill us. If we notice ourselves procrastinating or avoiding, we want to identify which kind of laziness is arising. If we can honestly self-reflect in this way, then applying the four allies and two strengths is natural, and we can move forward buoyed by our own clarity and inspiration.

There is a famous verse by Shantideva from the Diligence Chapter of *The Way of the Bodhisattva* that sums up the importance of learning to work with our lazy mindsets:

When they find a dying serpent,
Even crows behave like soaring eagles.
Therefore if I am weak and feeble-hearted,
Even little faults will strike and injure me.

If we don't address our negative habits and tendencies, if we just lie there inert, ignoring them or in denial, our negativities will fester and grow bigger and bigger. We need to muster a "can-do" mentality, along with some self-respect and self-confidence. We need to think positive thoughts to ourselves: *If others have done it, why not me?* It is all in the learning of traits, applying and adopting skillful means, and becoming more and more familiar with whatever it is that we wish to learn or engage or do. As Shantideva says in the Patience Chapter, "There is nothing that does not get easier with practice."

The power of familiarization should not be underestimated. Many of our habits are unconscious. We may think the problem is some intrinsic sense of low self-esteem or a lack of confidence, for instance, but in reality it is simply a repetitive, unconscious habitual reaction to something. We are blind to these habitual reactions and act out from that unconscious impulse. We have not yet learned how to counteract such a response with something like positive pride and confidence.

Confidence must be created. No one is born with it. It must be fostered through familiarization in the context and field of what we wish to accomplish. We do this by examining what our goals mean to us, what our purpose is in pursuing them, and what we stand to lose by not accomplishing them. Diligence is how we create confidence. It teaches us how to cultivate positive pride that counteracts our neuroses and develop self-respect regarding our ability to accomplish what we wish to do. This is all achieved through the process of repeated familiarization.

Many great masters have said, "If you have great diligence, you will attain enlightenment swiftly. If you have medium diligence, you will attain enlightenment accordingly. Those with a little diligence will attain enlightenment according to that. Without any diligence at all, there is no enlightenment or progress." Our level of accomplishment matches our level of tsöndru or diligence. This is true on the spiritual path, with conventional pursuits, and with any other endeavor we might pursue.

UNDERSTANDING INTENTION AND NEGATIVITY

When we aim to accomplish something, it is helpful to understand the impediments we are bound to face. How we respond to challenges greatly determines their outcome. Being aware of our response takes mindfulness, meaning we need to pay attention to the state of our mind. Mindfulness is a great friend that helps us stay on track. If we don't have some level of mindfulness, even neutral actions can tend toward the negative, as our thoughts can easily slip into judgment or a subtle level of disdain toward others, even those whom we do not personally know, or regarding situations that we only hear about through the news or other third-party sources.

On the bodhisattva path, our speech and the actions of our body are hugely influenced by the mind's intention or its "tone." So first and foremost, we want to pay attention to the tone of our mind, as that influences the direction of our speech, our physical actions, and, most importantly, our inner response and reactions. Shaping the tone and the intention of our mind does not happen by itself. It takes self-reflection, mindfulness, consciously valuing the importance of a positive mindset, and being open and ready to face the challenges that are sure to arise. If we learn how to shape our intention to be genuine and pure—meaning altruistic—our actions and speech will also be virtuous.

The Mahayana Buddhist teachings always emphasize that the main factor determining whether a deed is virtuous or harmful, positive or negative, is not necessarily the act itself, but rather the intention or motivation behind the act. Consider, for instance, if we were to encounter a deer running from a hunter, and the hunter should happen to come along and ask us, "Which way did the deer run?" If we point in the opposite direction and say, "That way," it would technically be a lie. Although lying is a negative deed, in this case the lie is motivated by a positive intention to save the deer's life, so the lie would be positive. The positive or negative nature of a physical or verbal deed is thus mainly determined by our intention. In the mind, however, there is absolutely no flexibility or excuse: what is negative is negative, and what is positive is positive.

How do we know whether our mind's intention is truly negative or truly positive? One way is to privately check in with ourselves and examine whether the goal in our mind is to benefit others. If it is, then the intention is generally good. On the other hand, if the goal is self-centered or self-serving on some level, even if it initially looks good or is seemingly virtuous and altruistic when perceived from the outside, the deed is considered negative, meaning it will bring a negative result to its agent.

What Makes Something Negative:
Four Observations

In our relative world, everything arises and occurs based on the natural law of cause and effect. In Buddhism, this is called karma. Karma simply means action, which includes both the cause and the effect. That action can be positive, negative, or somewhere in between. The mind's intention is the deciding factor that makes an action positive or negative. Any genuinely altruistic intention is based on knowing that all beings long for happiness and freedom from pain.

When we intentionally harm or hurt those who long for happiness, especially with a self-serving motivation, such an act is negative. All sentient beings want to be free from suffering just like us, so when we cause them pain, such acts are naturally unjust, or *marungpa* in Tibetan. According to the natural law of cause and effect, karma never misses. Unjust deeds always come back with consequences for the doer. Respecting this knowledge—in much the same way as we respect and abide by the "laws of the land" such as stopping at red lights—ensures our well-being.

The Buddha did not invent karma or cause and effect, nor did he dictate what was virtuous and what was nonvirtuous. He merely observed how the phenomenal world works, and thus discovered how cause and effect function. It is important to understand that when we say "negative," it is not because the Buddha himself deemed certain deeds to be negative. He did not say, "This is positive and this is negative because I say so," nor did he proclaim sets of commandments for people to follow in order to be "virtuous disciples." In the natural order of things, positive and negative deeds are not determined in such ways. Instead, the Buddha made four observations that serve as criteria for determining whether something may be considered negative. These four criteria are extremely useful to contemplate and to observe for ourselves.

The Buddha's first criterion for determining something as negative is that negative deeds and their root cause—self-centered neurosis—*create suffering*. In our experience they are painful. When we engage in unvirtuous or negative mindsets, we experience pain on some level. For instance, when we lash out in anger or rage, seethe with jealousy and envy, fixate on something with greed and attachment, are bewildered and confused as to how to proceed, or are puffed up with our own arrogance and self-importance, these are not pleasurable or peaceful feelings or emotions. They are uncomfortable or painful in our experience—they hurt, often quite viscerally. These states of mind are called *kleshas* or poisons because they contaminate our mind and consume us in pain. In Sanskrit, *klesha* literally means "poison." All beings innately wish to be happy, at ease, and at peace. Neurotic klesha states of mind and destructive emotions are the very opposite of that.

The second criterion the Buddha observed for determining something as negative is that all klesha activity, or neurosis, *veils the truth*. One of the most basic universal truths is that all beings wish to be happy and will work to secure the sources of that happiness. Alongside this, all beings wish to be free from any form of suffering and will work to avoid the sources of suffering. All of us, without exception, work on this twenty-four hours a day, seven days a week, even while sleeping and dreaming. Furthermore, in the absolute truth—or the true nature of the phenomenal world—there is no duality, no intrinsic self or other. Absolute truth is therefore always experienced as peace and equilibrium. As we indulge in negative states or kleshas like anger or greed, these qualities and the truth—both relative and absolute—are the furthest thing from our mind. Instead, our delusion is all-consuming, and we take the dualistic world to be very, very real.

When we get angry, it is said that our experience is largely made up of our own projections. In the klesha or neurosis of anger, we lose touch with the universal truth of the relative world, not to mention the peace and equilibrium of the emptiness view of absolute truth. Even as meditators, when we get caught up in extreme emotions, everything else is forgotten. What matters most is that we make our case, prove our point, win the argument, and get what we are fighting for. That becomes the priority. As we engage in negative mindsets, neuroses, or kleshas and solidify ourselves further in our self-absorption and self-justifying logic, we move further and further away from the truth, both relative and absolute. This then, is the second observation or reason why the Buddha identified neurosis as negative: it veils the truth.

The Buddha's third criterion identifying neurosis as negative is that it *increases its own kind*. If we get angry and lash out once, it is easier to do so the next time the urge arises. If we succumb to a craving and go for it, that action tends to increase our craving for the same thing even more. As a whole, our *sépa*, or desirous state of mind, increases the more we engage it. That is the nature of desire—it is insatiable and can never fully be satisfied or fulfilled. As the teachings say, giving in to sépa or craving is like drinking salty water: the more we drink, the thirstier we become. A lottery winner, for instance, might previously have been living in mediocre conditions, maybe even slightly on the rough side. After coming into a great deal of money, the person starts to buy all manner of things and gets used to that comfort and privilege. But there is never a cap to that. They want the next new thing; they want more and more and more. At some point, they can't tolerate even a fraction of the inconvenience they used to live with quite comfortably. If they have to sit in economy class on an airplane, it feels like going to a lower realm. They suffer greatly.

As we get attached to certain things and actively engage in that attached mindset, we sow the seeds for further attachment. This is due to the power of attachment's own force more than any other factor. It is no more mysterious than that. While in a state of craving, you can't also be content with what you have: two states of mind cannot coexist at the same time in one mind stream. Our modern culture has unfortunately fallen into a pit of craving, with sépa feeding more sépa. While engaged in this state of mind, we have no chance or room to find contentment and ease inside ourselves. The Buddha thus observed how unchecked neurosis or klesha activity self-proliferates endlessly, and this is therefore the third criterion that makes neurosis negative.

The fourth criterion for determining something as negative is that engaging in a negative deed with ill intent—whether in the mind, as speech, or as a physical action—sows a seed or leaves an imprint deep inside our *alaya*, or mind stream. When proper conditions arise, that imprinted or planted seed *ripens in the future as suffering* in the being's mind stream, physical body, or environment. Just as a single mango seed grows and matures into a huge tree producing thousands of fruits year after year for many, many years, the ripening and proliferating of negative seeds must likewise be endured.

It is extremely helpful to study these four criteria and understand what defines something as negative. As we can see, in Buddhism, negativity is not random or labeled based on the point of view of a higher power. Something is negative based on wisdom and observation. These four points of observation are given so that we can analyze our own experiences and thus gain firsthand knowledge of what is negative and what is positive.

In other religious traditions, I believe that teachings on virtue and nonvirtue, or advice on what to do and what not to do, come from the same wisdom as in Buddhism. In these traditions, however, advice on how to behave virtuously is often given without much exploration or explanation beyond that certain deeds are moral or immoral. The Buddha's teachings provide great and profound explanations on the nature and the functioning of the phenomenal world and the mind—such as what makes something negative. There is much to explore firsthand in the Buddhadharma, and the Buddha's teachings always appeal to one's own wisdom and personal experience. As the Buddha himself exhorted: "Examine my words like a goldsmith examines gold. Don't take my words as truth simply because they come from me."

How Habits Are Formed: Four Factors

It helps to remember, as Shantideva says, that everything is habit, both positive and negative. As all habits are formed, they can also be "unformed"—deconstructed or dismantled. Letting go of bad habits and forming positive ones is a process. Most negative habits are established unconsciously, and due to that lack of awareness they can become quite destructive. Our first priority is to become self-aware of our habits and patterns. We want to withhold judgment and learn to observe ourselves in these moments like a neutral but interested third party might do. This nonjudgmental observation creates a basis for us to change our behavior and therefore our habits, for habits are nothing more than compounded patterns of behavior that are created and uncreated. Our recognition of them can lead to their making and unmaking.

There are four factors that allow a habit to be formed or unformed. They apply to both positive and negative habits. The first factor that allows a habit to form is *repetition*. When we do something over and over again, it creates a brain pathway that makes it easier to repeat next time and the next time and so on. We all know how this works with negative habits, of course, but the same is true when creating positive habits. There is power in repetition—it just depends on whether it is in a positive, supportive direction or the opposite of that.

The second factor that allows a habit to take hold is *intensity*, meaning doing something in a heightened way, with more force than usual. Deeds leave an imprint based on their consistency and their force. We can observe these two factors in action across various areas of our lives and see for ourselves if they hold true for us in both positive and negative directions.

The third factor that contributes to something becoming a habit is the *lack of a counteragent*. This refers to doing something repeatedly or with force and without the presence of anything that might interfere with or stop that activity. On the negative side of things, this could refer to allowing ourselves to easily become irritated at the slightest provocation and never applying any self-reflection or *lojong*—meaning "mind training"—which could counter the flow of that activity, speech, or state of mind. On the positive side, it could be a commitment to rejoice whenever we encounter something that triggers feelings of jealousy. The lack of a counteragent here is our *not* giving in to the temptation of envy, and instead following through with rejoicing in the happiness or good fortune of others.

The fourth factor that allows a habit to form is the *availability of the field*. For instance, if someone is struggling with alcohol addiction and there are bottles of wine sitting in the cupboards at home, that is the availability of the field. Or, if we are working on developing our loving kindness practice, the availability of the field would be sentient beings and learning to consider them all as equal in their wish to be happy and free from suffering. The availability of the field refers to the material or substance to which we are habituating ourselves. It can be a physical substance or a mental area of interest. It is the subject matter of our habits, in both the positive direction and the negative.

Many of us feel stuck in our negative habits, but these four factors show us how dynamic and fluid habits are. We do not come into this world with the habits that we now have; they are not intrinsically with us from birth. Negative habits are formed unconsciously. They are things we have learned to do out of ignorance. Positive habits, on the other hand, need to be practiced with some effort and vision, and we therefore need to be patient with ourselves. Many people think that they are helpless in the face of their habits, and it can feel that way when there is a strong force to a habitual pattern that has built momentum over time. But habits are not intrinsic entities, and we are not helpless.

With regard to negative habits, applying the four factors that form habits in an opposite manner—that is, ceasing to engage the habit repeatedly or consistently, lowering the volume of our intensity if we do engage in the habitual activity, applying a counteragent when the habit is present, and removing the availability of the field—can dismantle almost any negative habit.

We have been habituated to our narrow self-absorption for a long time, so the activities of that mindset come quite easily to us. Like dropping a bucket down a well, it takes no effort. Gravity simply pulls the bucket to the bottom. We have all had the experience of saying hurtful things or acting out in ways that, when we look back, we can't fully comprehend: *Why did I do what I did, or say what I said?* In that moment, however, it seemingly just happened. In that moment it may even have felt good to say the hurtful thing that we said or lash out in the way that we did. In that moment, the force was just there, and we went with it. Most of our unvirtuous deeds, words, or thoughts are like this. It all comes so easily in the moment of our unconscious, habitually reactive mind. But remember, we are not helpless. We can put these four factors to the test as a way to begin forming positive habits and, likewise, apply the opposite of these four factors to slowly decrease the momentum of our negative habits.

CLAIMING YOUR DHARMA EDUCATION

When we first begin practicing self-reflection and mindfulness and try to turn our habitual reactions around to virtuous responses, it can all seem foreign and difficult. Where do we start? How do we know we are on the right track? It seems to require a tremendous amount of effort. This is why cultivating our Dharma education is critical.

Education always elevates humanity. Dharma education, in particular, imparts wisdom and perspective to whoever takes interest and applies themselves to study and practice. Unfortunately, we do not receive this kind of education in our mainstream conventional schooling, so we must seek it out and take up our own self-study. We are extremely fortunate that so many of the Buddha's teachings still survive in our world, that they have been preserved in Tibet and other countries, and that they are now being translated into Western languages. Studying Shantideva's teachings in one's own language, being able to access that level of intelligence and wisdom in an easily accessible book that you can keep on your own bookshelf or nightstand—this is the greatest inheritance for human beings of this age to claim.

In this light, we must strive to educate ourselves in the Dharma, so that we know how to accurately identify what causes pain and suffering for ourselves and others and, furthermore, recognize what supports us in building our own wisdom and discernment. Becoming more and more familiar with what supports us and where that brings us in the end versus what is harmful and keeps us stuck in the mire of our destructive habitual patterns—simply gaining that perspective alone is more than half the work.

Acquiring such perspective brings us tremendous freedom and floods us with deep abiding joy, because we realize that we have a choice. Joy comes from being free and recognizing the clarity of choice or agency. We only know that we have this choice, however, if we are willing to educate ourselves—if we are willing to go into our habitual neuroses or klesha mindsets and explore how they formed and from what driving force. In order to come out the other side, we have to be willing to go in. Only then are we eligible to genuinely discover more conscious and wholesome responses.

As we become more open and familiar with this internal process, we naturally develop new habits in place of the old ones. As new habits form and our experience changes, this process becomes easier and easier—we build momentum, which itself brings greater joy, motivating us to go further. After all, we are not doing this haphazardly or making it up as we go. This process is based on the wisdom of the Buddha and of great awakened, unconditionally compassionate beings like Shantideva. Through our education in the Dharma, our longing to awaken, and our willingness to transform, we can joyfully fulfill our potential as human beings.

THE DILIGENCE CHAPTER

1

Thus with patience I will strive with diligence.
For in such diligence enlightenment is found.
If no wind blows, then nothing stirs,
And neither is there merit without diligence.

This first verse in the Diligence Chapter of *The Way of the Bodhisattva* concisely identifies our need for diligence or joyful exertion in all we endeavor to accomplish.

What is this diligence or tsöndru? As we have started to explore, *diligence* is the characteristic of a delighted mind sustainably engaged in an activity—not just any random activity, though. Diligence refers to the force that allows us to engage in virtuous activities with a buoyant, resilient mind. The tone of the mind is joyful, and that joy in virtuous activity is precisely what helps sustain our engagement.

If there is no wind, a sailboat will not function. It will stay stagnant and motionless in the water or drift wherever the current flows.

Diligence is the wind that fills our sails and moves us forward on our path, supporting our progress in a positive, wholesome direction. Diligence or joyful exertion doesn't stand by itself; it is always in relation to something we are trying to do. As we work on developing qualities of virtue—for example, when engaging the paramitas of generosity, moral discipline, patience, meditation, and wisdom—we need the paramita, or perfection, of diligence to follow through with them. Diligence is not only necessary on the spiritual path, it is essential for seeing any worthy activity through to its completion.

There are, of course, many ways we can follow through with something. We can force ourselves to do things with a goal in our mind; we can trudge through our obligatory tasks, resenting every step, but plodding along nonetheless; we can "grin and bear it," pretending to like what we are doing but really just trying to get it finished so we can check it off our long to-do list. These examples all have a goal in mind requiring a certain kind of diligence, but this is not what the Buddha meant when he spoke of the perfection of diligence as the fourth paramita. That kind of diligence, which Shantideva expounds upon here in *The Way of the Bodhisattva*, has joy at its core. The paramita of diligence is a fully cognizant, joyful exertion toward the perfection of wisdom and compassion.

2

Diligence means joy in virtuous ways.
Its contraries have been defined as laziness,
An inclination for unwholesomeness,
Defeatism and self-contempt.

3

A taste for idle pleasure
And a craving for repose and sleep,
No qualms about the sorrows of samsara:
Laziness indeed is born from these.

Shantideva first identifies the joy that is integral to diligence, and then outlines the very thing that hinders the accomplishment of our aspirations: laziness. As we discussed, the Buddhist teachings identify three categories of laziness or internal obstacles that we can encounter in our life and on our path:

1. *Jéluk gi lélo*: Attachment to sleep, getting "rest," leisure time, or a yearning for idleness.
2. *Jawa ngenshen gyi lélo*: Attachment to mundane distractions, or the laziness of unwholesome ways.
3. *Daknyi nyépé lélo*: Habitual self-denigration, low self-esteem, self-loathing, or defeatism.

As we explore these obstacles in more detail, it is important to keep in mind that laziness itself is not necessarily the core issue—laziness is a symptom. The root of our laziness is our *shenpa*, or our unchecked, often unconscious preferences and attachments that extend into and pervade various activities and habits, preventing us from accomplishing what we wish. *Shenpa* is often translated as "attachment," but it is deeper than that. We often have a visceral, though largely unconscious, level of preference for how we want things to be. This preference can express itself as either attachment or aversion—the word *shenpa* can refer to either of these expressions. Before we become more conscious and mindful of our thoughts and emotions, our shenpa can reveal itself in various forms of dissatisfaction, restlessness, and distraction, which can translate into one of the three types of laziness.

One place our shenpa can manifest is our reluctance to honestly reflect upon impermanence and the suffering of samsara. For many of us there is a great deal of discomfort and fear in contemplating or taking these teachings to heart. As an example of this, we may for the moment be enjoying relative comfort and ease. Intellectually, of course, we know how quickly circumstances can change—we see this with others, we read about it in the news, and we may have already experienced this ourselves or through loved ones. Our shenpa or preferences, however, keep the possibility of impermanence and change at arm's length. We know that death is coming closer with each passing day, but instead of being realistic about this, we opt to numb out in distractions or avoidance or simply give up without even trying to do something meaningful with the rest of our lives.

In the Diligence Chapter, Shantideva encourages us to look at all of this with great candor, honesty, and humor. He continually points out the irony of how we live based on shenpa versus how we could live based on *bodhichitta*, or a mindset of awakening and joy.

1

JOY

As the verses unfold, we will continually discover the notion of joy being emphasized as an indispensable aspect of diligence. This makes tremendous sense. If we enjoy something, we will want to keep doing it and will keep coming back for more. This is true both in conventional life and on the spiritual path. In the latter, joy sustains us along the journey of awakening. It is the joy of holding the greater perspective of what we are doing, and it is the joy of knowing how each step of the path fits into this larger picture of awakening. Furthermore, there is the joy of being present with each moment of our mind's awareness and its application of virtue. Perhaps the greatest source of joy on the spiritual path is our Dharma education and the wisdom we gain from integrating what we learn from the teachings with our personal self-reflection and experience—that is, learning to make a "two-handed clap." This integration of the Dharma with our life gives us an ever deepening and broadening perspective on what we are doing with our life.

Genuinely understanding what we are doing and why unleashes tremendous energy, inspiration, and, ultimately, joy. Here, in *The Way of the Bodhisattva*, it is the joy of engaging in the practice of the four immeasurables and bodhichitta—in other words, the joy of progressing in our practice of altruism, loving kindness, and compassion for the benefit of all beings—and the joy of accumulating authentic wisdom and the positive energy of merit, all based on the Buddha's teachings and our own intelligence.

Just as a glass chimney protects the flame of a lantern on a windy day, diligence protects the flame of our practice from the unpredictable winds of distraction, preoccupation, laziness, and defeatism. These are the elements that can easily extinguish the lamp of our awakening. The second and third verses of the Diligence Chapter introduce us to these elements. These elements are internal tendencies that can become obstacles on our path, the winds that threaten the flame of our awakening. Shantideva brings up the obstacles at the beginning of the chapter, as these are what we will be working with as we put time and effort into our path—or into anything we sincerely wish to accomplish.

I always marvel that what applied to our human mind and neuroses 1,200 years ago, or 2,600 years ago when the Buddha was alive, still applies to our modern, or perhaps postmodern, mindset. Even in the midst of our technological and scientific advances, the way our minds function, our neuroses, what threatens our well-being, and what helps us move through and overcome our negative habitual patterns are all still basically the same. The makeup of our human mind has not changed much over the centuries. This is why the Buddha's wisdom is so effective and profound and still has relevance.

2

THE THREE CATEGORIES
OF LAZINESS

We will now explore the three kinds of laziness in detail. These themes run throughout the verses of the Diligence Chapter, so we want to thoroughly familiarize ourselves with them.

JÉLUK GI LÉLO: THE LAZINESS
OF YEARNING FOR IDLENESS

The first kind of laziness or obstacle is *jéluk gi lélo*, which is our attachment to sleep, the idea that we need "rest," or as it is translated here, "a yearning for idleness." We all have a lot of attachment or shenpa in this area. One reason we are attached to sleep is that when we are sleeping, our gross thoughts and emotions and perceptions dissolve. It is a bit like being drugged. It is a break from our day-to-day life and its stresses. Of course, we all need a certain amount of wholesome sleep in order to stay healthy and well. Physically, from a medical point of view, seven to eight hours of sleep is what an adult needs. His Holiness the Fourteenth Dalai Lama says that he sleeps soundly for eight hours each night. In the old days, many teachers slept just two or three hours a night, but now the standard is longer. This is not the kind of sleep or rest that Shantideva is addressing as jéluk gi lélo.

Here, Shantideva points out the extra element of our *attachment* to sleep or being idle, the draw of the anesthesia of these experiences and our reluctance to wake up and get to our meditation cushion or engage in whatever is most meaningful. In that extra forty-five minutes or half-hour of sleep that we fight for with the snooze button, we lose time for our morning meditation practice or to collect and center ourselves. Instead of getting up with a fresh feeling, we struggle and cling to a few extra minutes of sleep, which only ends up making us rushed and flustered throughout the rest of the morning. That is jéluk gi lélo, which literally translates as "the heaviness of laziness."

This first category of laziness is in the context of our internal resistance to exerting effort to overcome the challenges to achieving whatever it is that we wish to accomplish.

How We Relate to Pressure

Much of our laziness—particularly this first kind, but also applying to all three categories—has to do with how we relate to pressure in life. Whenever we wish to accomplish something meaningful, we also feel a certain amount of pressure. People generally take one of two approaches in relation to pressure. The first and more ideal approach is that we accept and welcome pressure. We meet it, knowing that it is part of getting to anything worthwhile. In this approach, we embrace the challenge and feel ready to face whatever is ahead. We aim to turn that process into joy. If from a young age we have trained in a certain sport, for instance, there is naturally pressure, but we learn to strive, accept the pressure, and overcome any challenges with vigor and enthusiasm—especially if we truly want to excel in that sport.

In Brazil, as in many other countries, most boys and many girls begin playing soccer as soon as they can walk. To make it as a professional soccer player, like Ronaldo Nazário, takes diligence and vision. His diligence and vision are what pulled him out of bed early in the morning for practice every single day—not just for a few months, or a year or two, but for many years. He learned to face pressure with joy. And, of course, there was also sacrifice—like not always being able to join his friends in what they were doing. But knowing that consistency would enable him to achieve his dream, he made those sacrifices, trading them for the joy of a larger accomplishment.

Our chance of success in any field comes with the willingness to train. Training, even if it is hard and comes with pressure, must be inspired by the larger vision of what we wish to accomplish—and by the joy in training, in facing challenges, and in achieving the vision that one is aiming for. It is not sufficient to simply be good at something. That is only the beginning. We must reinspire ourselves over and over again, knowing that if we make aspirations and apply ourselves, step-by-step we will get where we want to go. This is how people achieve what they wish and become supremely competent at what they do, reaping the fruit of their efforts not just once but throughout their lifetime and beyond. Outside of this, there is no great mystery or secret to success or to achieving what one wishes to accomplish.

The second approach we could take in relation to pressure could apply, for example, to a person who loves sports and loves the idea of becoming a world-renowned gymnast or tennis player. Many children have this kind of fantasy, but it usually remains just a fantasy. Why? There are many variables, of course, but one common factor is our reaction to pressure. Many of us freeze in the face of it. We can't think of how to proceed because we are overwhelmed by the sensation of pressure. Instead of working with our mind and sensations, we react to our discomfort and reject it. This kind of reaction is itself a habit that has likely formed early in life. It can be helpful to try to trace the origins of this response in order to better understand what is happening. Nonetheless, our reactiveness robs us of our intelligence, our creativity, our ability to weigh the pros and cons, and it deprives us of our joy in meeting whatever challenges may arise.

Instead of creatively and joyfully finding a way forward, we opt for the so-called easy path: we give up. In giving up, we are, in fact, still seeking joy. But rather than cultivating our vision, strength, and diligence, we go for the deceptive, short-term joys of sleeping in, avoiding sacrifices or challenges, and essentially caving in to the discomfort of feeling pressure. In so doing, we never realize our dream of being a great gymnast or tennis player or whatever it was that we held as meaningful and loved to do. Instead, we hang out with our pals at the mall or play video games, and soon these things become more our lifestyle than striving for our initial aspiration, wish, or fantasy.

Lélo or laziness always indicates that there is something more meaningful that we wish to do. It can be in the back of our minds or in the fore, but we are avoiding it or procrastinating. Dogs sleeping all day are not lélo—they just do what they do and that is it. They are not sleeping to get away from anything. Lélo is for humans when we have something to do, but, for whatever reason, we don't do it. When we are sick and therefore can't do something important, that is also not lélo. Lélo is when we want to and we can, but we don't. This first kind of laziness is thus an aversion to and a rejection of exertion—of rising to the occasion or to life itself. We use sleep or idleness as an excuse to avoid exertion, particularly meaningful exertion. Ironically, we manage to get to work on time or be prompt with our dental appointments, but when it comes to getting to our cushion or to other meaningful activities, we often give in to this type of laziness.

Jéluk means heavy, and *lélo* is laziness. Jéluk gi lélo is when we become heavy, and then heavier and heavier, as we give in to our idleness, resistance, and lethargy. Succumbing to these is jéluk gi lélo. Nothing is accomplished when we surrender to this, other than maybe getting more rest or sleep. Pursuing diligence makes us agile, light, and able to apply ourselves as we wish. Giving in to jéluk gi lélo does the opposite.

In contemplating all of this, we must not make the mistake of thinking that those who have learned to work with pressure and balance their workload—who have been able to inspire themselves, work with challenges, and fulfill their vision—have never thought of sleeping in or slacking off. The same feelings that arise for us also arise for them. The difference is that they recognize the risks of going down the path of laziness, use that awareness as a way to inspire themselves to continue, and make a habit of this. They focus on their goal and consciously remind themselves of what it means to them. This gives them the oomph to face obstacles. In doing so, they learn to take genuine joy in working with the pressure that they feel, in navigating their workload, and in meeting challenges with increasing confidence and ease.

The joy of working with pressure increases as it comes more fully from our own self-motivation. Any progress we make speaks for itself, and each step on the journey fulfills us. Success does not depend only on skill or ability, though these things are also important factors. The most critical factor to success in any field is how we work with our mental states, our arising emotions and sensations, and how we overcome the internal challenges that we are sure to face. Our shenpa to sleep and being idle is the first obstacle to diligence.

JAWA NGENSHEN GYI LÉLO: THE LAZINESS OF ATTACHMENT TO MUNDANE DISTRACTIONS

The second type of laziness is our attachment to mundane activities, in Tibetan *jawa ngenshen gyi lélo*. These are distracting activities, habituated patterns, and our addiction to small, meaningless "pleasures." We all know this type of laziness: of getting hooked into and lulled by mundane tasks, diversions, and distracting preoccupations and using them as a means to procrastinate. If these small, unimportant things were all that we wanted to accomplish or cared to do with our lives, then this would not be lélo or laziness. But we generally have higher aspirations, more important or valuable things on our mind that we wish to accomplish. We know that these aspirations won't be realized or evolve on their own. Yet we often have a hard time letting go of our jawa ngenshen gyi lélo, the various distractions that eat up all our time.

For the sake of these small pleasures, we waste a tremendous amount of each day. We get up, take a shower, make our coffee, start checking our phone or computer, answer messages, look at the news, take a walk, clean the house, rearrange the furniture, think about what we will have for dinner, do some gardening, lie down on the couch, go to the beach, get on Amazon and search for something to buy, read a book, scroll through Instagram, watch Netflix, clean the house again, and so on.

This is called *dudzi* in Tibetan. Dudzi refers to meaningless activities that, in reality, are a form of avoiding what we need or want to do. We are attached to the mildly numbing "bliss" of various dudzi and find it difficult to disengage ourselves and get onto the meditation cushion or move on to doing something meaningful. There is an element of addiction here. Dudzi can be any number or variety of occupations, but they all have the distinctive flavor of distraction, fueled by our shenpa to numb out or procrastinate.

Of course, we must pay our bills and keep our home tidy—doing such things is not jawa ngenshen gyi lélo. *Jawa* means "activities," *ngen* means "insignificant," and *shen* refers to the attachment to doing such things. Pointing out the laziness of distracting preoccupations is not about the external activities, per se; it is revealing an internal habit or pattern of relating. We can become addicted to various dudzi activities and use them as a means of avoiding working on what is meaningful to us. We do this for various reasons, which can differ from person to person. For some it is a way of avoiding pressure, as we spoke of before. Others develop a taste for the tension of avoidance—they become addicted to the stress of putting things off. And for still others, occupying oneself with various dudzi activities can become a way of justifying their existence. It is called lélo, or laziness, because these dudzi activities prevent us from doing what we truly wish to do.

One of the most seductive and addictive forms of jawa ngenshen gyi lélo is being locked onto a screen, whether our TV, our computer, our tablet, or especially our phone. This is a good example of the "availability of the field" in terms of how habits are formed. Nowadays, we can scroll through the internet and watch anything we want, for as long as we want, all from our phone, which most of us are never without—that field is thus always available. We don't have to be home, planted on the couch at 8 p.m. every Thursday to watch our favorite show for an hour. Those days are long gone. In addition to watching shows or scrolling through social media, there are many other forms of this kind of lélo. Despite how easy and attractive these activities are, no one is going to be truly fulfilled having spent half of their life glued to a little screen. We nonetheless lose many hours every day, week, and month in just this way.

Insisting on rearranging our furniture while our house is on fire would not be wise. Similarly, while impermanence is staring us in the face, it doesn't make sense to spend our time lost in distracting preoccupations. It is not that we don't get small momentary pleasures out of our dudzi. Distracting ourselves can be enjoyable in the short term or as a way of coping with situations on some level. But, if these small pleasures prevent us from being productive in our conventional or Dharmic pursuits, our chances of accomplishment, success, and personal fulfillment gradually fade away.

In order to overcome this, we must be willing to confront our attachment to our dudzi—to honestly self-reflect on our internal habits of avoidance and procrastination—and the self-perpetuating nature of attachment itself. We must want to ask ourselves: *Why am I afraid of letting go of these things?* Even if we do find a bit of joy and satisfaction from zoning out in our distractions, overindulging in them does not support us. Furthermore, we can end up sabotaging ourselves as procrastination and overindulgence prevent us from relating to our deeper aspirations in a sane and healthy way.

We must thus take a moment to reflect that time is short. We are not here forever. Everyone will soon pass from this world—including ourselves. Spending so much time in the morning getting our coffee or tea just right, getting lost in our devices, and squandering our precious moments to practice or to sit quietly and center our mind and body in its natural state—we must not let our life simply slip by in sheer distraction. It is helpful to induce a bit of fear in order to shake ourselves loose from the oppressive habit of procrastination. We should think, *I have to die; what will that be like? It could happen today, suddenly and unexpectedly. How will that be for me—am I ready to face that?* Such thoughts bring perspective and can dampen the momentum of our distracting preoccupations. This type of laziness is the second obstacle to developing diligence or joyful exertion.

DAKNYI NYÉPÉ LÉLO: THE LAZINESS OF SELF-DISPARAGEMENT

The third kind of laziness is *daknyi nyépé lélo*, which means the "laziness of habituated self-denigration." This form of laziness may surprise you. It is the subtlest and possibly the most difficult to identify and overcome. This explanation of self-denigration and low self-esteem is coming from the point of view of the Buddhist teachings, so it might feel like a new way of looking at these tendencies. It is helpful to keep an open mind and gently explore this in your own experience.

This third obstacle to joyful exertion or diligence is identified by how we have learned to habitually undermine ourselves with chronic self-loathing. In this context specifically, we use our low self-esteem to disengage—to avoid having to rise to the occasion and do what needs to be done. We use this tendency as an excuse to sink further down into the hole we are already in, and then sink further still. We think it is too hard to climb out, and we will probably fail anyway—so it's better to just stay where we are.

Self-denigration is interesting. It seems contrary to the ego, but in reality it can be a more inflated form of ego than what we normally perceive ego to be. It is still ego-clinging but in a negative light. The habit of self-denigration, which develops unconsciously, sits in the background saying, *I can't. Others can, but not me. I am not worthy, I am not able, so I may as well not even try.*

Thoughts are like fire, and emotions are like the smoke from that fire. Therefore, just as these thoughts arise, a rush of emotions—feeling incapable, insecure, and inadequate—also floods our chest. In all these thoughts and emotions, the sense of self is not diminished but rather enforced. This is not in a positive way, of course, but in a negative way. We can develop this internal way of relating to our world in the context of our work, our abilities, our overall potential, and the vision we may have for our lives. When we have not resolved these feelings and the thought processes that drive them, they can crop up all over the place, undermining and tricking us into thinking we are unworthy or unable do things.

Thoughts arise like passing clouds or a flowing river—there is no stopping them. There is no way to quarantine our mind or halt our thoughts and the subsequently arising emotions. If we do not solidify and grasp at them too much, however, our thoughts and emotions are not a problem, whatever they may be. It is when our state of mind becomes rigid or tight, rather than free-flowing, that our ability to skillfully apply ourselves is affected. We can become stuck in this solid state, learn to identify ourselves with that state, and then come to believe that this is who we are. We make excuses for ourselves and no longer strive to apply our mind and work with our developed habitual patterns. We slip into making fewer demands on ourselves, which, over time, makes us feel less and less capable. As this state of being becomes more familiar, the identity of "I can't" becomes more comfortable. We eventually resist doing anything to counter our developed identity of daknyi nyépé, or self-denigration.

This is not done consciously—it all happens in the unconscious. It is, nonetheless, a cunning excuse of ego to not have to exert or strive or change. It is an effective method of self-protection because we make it clear to ourselves and others that no demands should be placed upon us, and we should not have to meet expectations. We have already decided on this before we even try to exert ourselves. And if we do try and then fail, or have tried and failed in the past, instead of getting back up and trying again we use that failure to reinforce our daknyi nyépé. Eventually, whenever something doesn't simply fall into our lap or come easily to us, we feel entitled to pull back, extract ourselves, and say, "I can't."

The laziness of self-denigration can develop even further. When someone does something for another person, the natural response is to reciprocate on some level, even if just by feeling appreciation. Consciously we know that nothing happens as a one-handed clap, in the sense that no one can function all alone in the world. We are all dependent on one another to survive and function. When we give into the laziness of low self-esteem, the "I can't" mentality can solidify into a hard line of self-protectiveness, which we justify as a means to ignore any kind of reciprocation. This approach has a subtle level of aggression toward the world. It is not an overt aggression, but the edge of self-protection pushes everything else away. If anyone happens to expect anything from us, we feel threatened. This can be directed at our spouse, parents, friends, teachers, the community or society at large, or anyone with whom we have an interdependent relationship.

This dynamic can isolate us even further, reinforcing our defeatism and self-contempt.

When we become caught in this kind of self-absorption and isolation, we often end up comparing ourselves with others, particularly with those who have achieved whatever it is we would like to have in our lives. Without taking into account the karma of that other person—meaning that person's personal circumstances and the steps they have taken to achieve their goal—along with the challenges they inevitably faced in order to succeed, we focus only on the result or our projection of the result. In this tunnel vision of jealous comparison, we set ourselves up for constant failure. This, in turn, perpetuates the habit to further indulge in the laziness of low self-esteem and self-denigration, and it gets easier and easier to think that there is no choice.

No one wants to be lazy. It is a painful and oppressive state, as these three categories clearly illustrate. The pain and oppression of laziness are often compounded because we don't know where to begin to address them. There is resistance to looking squarely and honestly at our experience and to being present and curious regarding what we are feeling. It is too uncomfortable to face ourselves internally, so we avoid our feelings and procrastinate further.

To practice diligence in any field, we must be willing to work with our internal challenges and identify our neuroses—even open to getting well acquainted and friendly with them. Shantideva's teachings reveal and identify our inner psychological and emotional states so that we can become well acquainted and friendly with our challenges and neuroses.

The point of becoming aware of our own neuroses and obstacles is not to stew in them and make ourselves feel worse; the point is to remedy them. These neuroses are not "you," after all; they are an obstacle to you. They are an impediment to what you aspire to be and who you truly are. We aspire to be liberated and compassionate, not bound by our habitual reactiveness or prejudices. In acknowledging and understanding our neuroses, we naturally take the next step toward employing wisdom and skillful means. This doesn't happen just because we want it to. We need to be interested and willing to get in there and understand the impediment in order to then apply the remedy. To "get out," we have to "go in"—to explore the neurosis and precisely understand what is happening in our own experience. This creates room for wisdom and skillful means, or *tabshé* in Tibetan, to naturally arise. This is how we discover and apply the practice of diligence. There is tremendous joy in this process because along the way we come to know who we truly are.

3

IN ORDER TO GET OUT,
WE HAVE TO GO IN

Our Internal Dialogue

Humans have an astonishing tendency to forget lessons learned from past painful experiences, especially emotional ones. No matter how much we suffer in life due to our destructive emotions, self-importance, wrong deeds, karma, and laziness, in many ways we never learn. We get burned, we suffer, and then we do it all over again. We often have trouble identifying and then giving up what causes us pain. In order to rise up out of this confusion, we must determine how to have a constructive internal dialogue with ourselves.

We all possess the ability to know. We have a sense of what we need to adopt and what we need to get rid of or abandon. This general knowing of what is supportive to our well-being is part of our mind and awareness. This natural level of knowing, however, must be energized and clarified by our constructive internal thought processes. This means we must actively examine why we should do certain things and why it is good for us to proceed in such and such a way. Or why something is not good for us and what the outcome of clinging to that thing might be. Consciously analyzing such positive or negative potential results elevates our mind, helps us to realize our potential, and moves us forward effectively. Without our own conscious analysis of situations or experiences, we often end up blindly following whatever our surrounding culture tells us to aim or settle for.

Activating a constructive inner dialogue and thought process clarifies and gives weight to what we may already know or vaguely sense. This constructive thought process is based on *dradön drédzin gyi tokché*, in Tibetan, which means joining the mental image and mental label of any particular thing and forming a clear understanding about that topic. This constructs the foundation for accurate analysis and a deeper understanding of any topic we wish to consider. Clear understanding is brought to the forefront of our mind and generates supportive emotions that then guide us forward. Dradön drédzin gyi tokché and constructive thinking are thus a powerful generator of motivation, passion, and will.

Our attachment to doing things or staying busily distracted often keeps us from being curious about our mind or pursuing an inner dialogue and developing clarity. Our attachments can prevent us from being present with ourselves and directly discovering what that might be like. As a way to ground ourselves and be more present, it is always helpful to reflect upon impermanence—the impermanence of our life and all life, especially in light of our distracting preoccupations. One day we will all pass from this world; that is inevitable. At that time, what can we truly rely on? Not this body, not our distractions, and not our endless to-do lists. What will make the most difference for us in that crucial moment is the clarity of our understanding and, most especially, the positivity we have accumulated in our life, meaning our altruism toward others and the freedom and ease that this brings to our mind.

Verses 4–14, which will be explored here and in the coming chapters, address cultivating awareness of the laziness that yearns for idleness and sleep.

4
Snared by the trapper of defiled emotion,
Enmeshed and taken in the toils of birth,
Again you've strayed into the maw of Death.
What is it? Have you still not understood?

5

Don't you see how, one by one,
Death has come for all your kind?
And yet you slumber on so soundly,
Like a buffalo beside its butcher.

Impermanence comes for one and all. Every living being must face this, either harshly by force or gently by choice. We want our internal dialogue to remind us of the impermanence of life and let that fact sink in a little deeper each time. This will slowly shape how we relate to our distractions and laziness.

There is a traditional comparison of our life to those of animals held in the courtyard of a slaughterhouse, awaiting their fate. This may seem like an extremely morbid way to think about life, but if we openly reflect upon it, in many ways we can see how true it is. However long an animal is waiting in the courtyard or however long a fish is swimming within the fisherman's net, it is only a matter of time before the inevitable occurs. Even though each animal in the slaughterhouse courtyard or in the net has no destiny other than death, they are all oblivious to this fact. Most of the time so are we.

Reflecting quietly, we remind ourselves that, even as we watch our friends, partners, parents, grandparents, relatives, and other acquaintances continuously pass from this world, we rarely think that we ourselves might be next. Just like the animals in the courtyard or the fish in the nets, our minds are dull—we don't completely comprehend what is happening all around us. For the animals about to be slaughtered, perhaps this dullness prevents them from being terrified and anxious in those moments before; at least it seems that way to us. But I think animals also fear death and anxiously anticipate their demise. My mother used to live near a slaughterhouse in Nepal. She would tell us that, when the buffaloes were brought in on trucks, she could see that they had tears streaming down their faces. Maybe they sensed what was about to happen to them. The point is, if we do not comprehend that we will soon pass from this life, we are worse off than the most oblivious, dull-witted animal waiting in line at the slaughterhouse.

4

CONTEMPLATING IMPERMANENCE SUPPORTS THE PRACTICE OF VIRTUE

You might be wondering, *If I am going to die, what is the point of thinking about it so much? Why not worry about it when it comes?* The purpose of contemplating death, impermanence, and the uncertainty of the time and circumstance of our passing is to motivate us toward virtue. Learning to cultivate virtuous deeds and a positive, altruistic mindset brings tremendous benefit to our present life and will also be a great force and support that we can count on while transitioning from this life into the next. We thus want to joyfully motivate ourselves toward contemplating impermanence and the value of practicing virtue and altruism.

Diligence can be applied to anything, positive or negative. Here we are applying our diligence to learning about virtue and the path of the bodhisattva. Contemplating impermanence grounds us and brings our mind into focus so we can develop a wholesome and supportive perspective, particularly regarding the cultivation of virtue.

To understand the meaning of virtue, we must first acknowledge that the mind is the most important factor in determining what is or isn't virtuous. To emphasize this, Shantideva continually exhorts us to take an attitude of delight toward engaging in virtue. If we are begrudgingly virtuous or only seemingly altruistic, that is not the practice of virtue. Virtue and altruism are truly positive when the mind is deeply delighted and joyful while engaged in positive deeds.

Only we can assess this internal difference. If we find that we are resentful or feel pressured to "do good," we should pause and honestly reflect on what is happening inside of us. It is important to take the time to properly investigate and relate to any unprocessed issues or currents flowing inside the mind. If we try to ignore, suppress, or deny such currents, they can end up derailing the best of our efforts and intentions. As we come to recognize that the mind's attitude is the most important factor in determining the outcome of our deeds, we learn to enjoy assessing where our mind is. Letting go of any lurking resentments and grudges, we become free to take genuine delight in virtuous deeds and altruism.

Working for the benefit of others—motivated by altruism and a good heart—ensures others' well-being and brings us confidence and satisfaction. Genuine delight in virtuous deeds grows from this personal experience. That delight need not be a physical sensation. It can simply be our knowledge and conviction that we and all sentient beings are deeply connected. If something works for all sentient beings, or as many as possible, it ultimately works for us as well. Deeds coming from this personal knowledge and understanding can be joyful because our wisdom is in control, not our neurosis. Deeds springing from genuine wisdom define positive action. Having confidence in this satisfies and delights us. We recognize that working for others assures our own happiness—or even *is* our own happiness. Doing something for others is ultimately doing something for oneself. This clarity inspires our heart toward delight in virtue.

If, on the other hand, something works for us but comes at the expense of others' well-being, even if we experience some temporary pleasure or gain, we ultimately end up paying for this imbalance. That is the natural law of cause and effect or karma. We can take this a step further and reflect that, when we are caught up in our distractions or a preoccupied mindset, we often don't have the presence of mind to respond to others as we wish. If something happens or someone says something that catches us off guard, we may automatically react from a self-centered emotional state. In that reaction, we often end up perpetuating confusion or bringing things to a painful point.

5

EXCITEMENT VERSUS
GENUINE DELIGHT

It is helpful to discern the difference between excitement and genuine happiness or delight. Genuine happiness or delight is a state of mind that is open and at ease, free of fear and anxiety. When we do something for others and feel happy about it, we don't experience much fear or anxiety. On the other hand, when we try to do something only for ourselves and are excited or even thrilled about it, if we observe the quality of our feelings, we will likely notice some level of anxiety. Underneath the thrill or excitement is hope and fear—hope that our action will work out and fear that it might not. Anxious grasping to get what we want and worry over the possibility of disappointment are usually there simultaneously, or one is just around the corner from the other.

If we are truly honest with ourselves, we may observe that getting what we were so excited to obtain doesn't prove to be as fulfilling as we had imagined. Even if we win the lottery, our excitement will likely be mixed with some measure of anxiety or shakiness—as if not quite standing on solid ground. Interestingly, such excitement is generally regarded as the experience of happiness. Culturally, we are influenced to regard this kind of adrenaline-infused thrill as a state of happiness or delight.

The human mind is quite susceptible to the addict's mindset. That mindset projects happiness and joy onto possessing or joining with the substance to which we are addicted. We can become self-absorbed in the drive to obtain that substance, whatever it may be. Unfortunately, happiness is never found in the object of our craving, and self-focused fixations or excitements never seem to live up to what we want or expect of them—or hardly last long enough to properly experience and enjoy. For addicts, the joy of getting high from a substance never truly fulfills them, and the brief experience of bliss only leaves them wanting more. Our sépa mindset is just like this: the excitement and "happiness" of an addict. Like an addict, we go for the objects of our craving again and again, despite them never being what we thought them to be. Our actions and intentions therefore do not meet.

One of my teachers, Nyoshul Khen Rinpoche, said, "True happiness cannot be found through great effort and willpower, but is already present in open relaxation and letting go." We find happiness when our mind and heart are open, present, and grounded in genuine altruism. From that grounded good heart and positive intention, acting for the good of others truly fulfills us, gives us confidence and satisfaction, and feeds our soul. When others are fulfilled by our good deeds, we are also fulfilled. When we positively affect others with our good heart, we are likewise affected.

Perhaps there is not much excitement in this approach—no great rush of adrenaline or thrill at the novelty of something new and different—but neither is there fear, anxiety, craving, or the inevitable letdown and shakiness of disappointment, leading to nothing else but starting all over again. On the other hand, the genuinely settled, wholesome delight of virtue, of acting for the welfare of others, sustains and fulfills us. This is the sort of delight and joy that Shantideva speaks of throughout the Diligence Chapter and the whole of *The Way of the Bodhisattva*.

Perhaps there are other kinds of happiness besides altruism and being virtuous and kind toward others—like having personal wealth, power, and the admiration and affection of other people. Maybe so. But in those cases, we have to continually remind ourselves or be confirmed that *I am rich, I am powerful, I am admired.* Happiness gained in this way depends largely on others' perceptions of us. It is not naturally abiding or dependable; we live at the whim of how others perceive us. Another problem with this kind of happiness is that arrogance and attachment can set in. With arrogance goes the ever-present fear and anxiety over losing our status, influence, wealth, or the admiration of others. We feel we must protect what we have, what we are proud of, or what we are attached to.

The grounded happiness of altruism is not like this. Wishing for the happiness of others with no strings attached is not necessarily fixated on a desired outcome. Developing an altruistic intention sustains our mind in a condition of well-being and happiness, regardless of what happens on the outside. His Holiness the Dalai Lama often says that, if we really want happiness, the best way to achieve it is to genuinely wish for others to be happy. This abiding altruistic intention is what we work on and cultivate with diligence on our path and in our life. Even though our positive intention is directed outward, our resultant well-being and happiness do not depend on the object at which they are directed. They are almost entirely dependent on the state of our own mind, heart, and intention.

If we attend to our good heart and diligently cultivate positive intentions, happiness is ours. Furthermore, when things do not work out, we are not dejected. We realize that everything has its own causes and conditions, and we cannot, like a wizard, control the outcome of everything. We can, however, maintain our own good heart and our positive intention. Whatever the outcome, our altruistic motivation and intention bring us delight or "bliss." Whatever happens, however karma unfolds for others, for ourselves, and for the world around us, on an inner level we enjoy bliss upon bliss. Not blissed-out blissy-bliss, but the direct, grounded experience of connecting with our own nature and our own good heart, which has the room to accept and work with everything that arises. If we want this kind of sustainable joy to accompany our endeavors, we must ground ourselves in altruism. Diligently working on this is within our control, and this is what keeps us buoyant, lighthearted, and happy.

6

THE POWER OF TRAINING THE MIND WITH POSITIVE INTENTIONS

Introducing the Four Immeasurables

In our discussion of laziness and diligence, we are exploring what brings us true and lasting fulfillment, joy, and peace. The Buddhist teachings have a structured and measured approach to establishing the ground for the practice of altruism and virtue. Without altruism and virtuous aspirations, it is difficult to find more than fleeting moments of fulfillment, joy, and peace.

Teachings on the four immeasurables—love, compassion, sympathetic joy, and equanimity—allow us to train our mind, explore the capacity of our heart, and develop authentic altruism and sanity. The four immeasurables are the nitty-gritty of bodhichitta practice—they are the "how to" when we talk about learning to unconditionally love others . . . and ourselves. As an inner practice, the core contemplations of the four immeasurables are loving kindness and compassion. Shaping our motivation toward securing beings' happiness, understanding the causes and conditions of how to do that, and knowing how to increase this further is the practice of loving kindness. Understanding how to help free beings from suffering and the causes and conditions that bind them to suffering and how to increase that freedom is the practice of compassion. The content our thoughts and emotions generate toward securing others' happiness and freeing them from suffering is the practice of bodhichitta.

The practice of bodhichitta—or loving kindness and compassion—must be free of prejudice and judgment. To ensure this, equanimity practice digs up our hidden prejudices, judgments, and grudges and brings forth the strength of principle. Rather than being motivated by emotion or personal preferences, equanimity, as the primary principle of both loving kindness and compassion, extends equally to whoever is sentient, whoever has a mind, whoever feels joy or pain. All sentient beings—all who are inherently sensitive to the experiences of happiness and suffering and who instinctually feel the wish to be happy and free from pain—are worthy objects of our love and compassion. Therefore, we approach loving kindness and compassion practices based on the principle and the immeasurable practice of equanimity. We do not choose one person over another, one culture or race over another, or one species over another. In the practice of bodhichitta or the four immeasurables, our intention and our altruism extend equally to all sentient beings.

Partiality, inequality, and the consequences arising from a self-centered mindset all revolve around our self-importance, *dak ché dzin* in Tibetan. The godfather of our emotional or intellectual self-centeredness is self-importance. In that setup, the ego, the self, and the self's preferences (shenpa) are always number one. Everything else is secondary. The immeasurable practice of sympathetic joy, of rejoicing in the successes of all beings, large and small, significant or otherwise, is thus essential to securing our loving kindness, compassion, and equanimity practices. Sympathetic joy secures our brave heart of bodhichitta because it exposes our conscious and unconscious tendencies of jealousy and competitiveness.

This is extremely helpful, because one minute we might wish someone well with a great flood of loving kindness or wish them to be free from suffering, but the next thing we know, we can find ourselves flooded with subtle or not so subtle feelings of competitiveness and envy. We might, for instance, see someone having something that we want, or we may secretly feel that person does not deserve whatever it is they have; we may suddenly feel that we have to compete with them in order to keep up on some level. Any of these conditions can arise, almost as if out of the blue. Before we catch ourselves, our competitiveness or envy automatically surges, and we can find ourselves wishing that this person be reduced to ashes and eradicated from the planet. This can happen among family members and old friends, and even between parents and children. It can happen with strangers, of course, but it is not uncommon between those who share love for one another. To prevent this and to instead secure our principle of love and compassion, our equanimity, good heart, and our altruistic intentions, we must practice the immeasurable of sympathetic joy. Sympathetic joy takes our bodhichitta practice to another level—a more reliable and well-processed level.

We will now explore the four immeasurables in detail as an actual practice we can do on a daily basis to exercise our diligence and altruism. Even though loving kindness and compassion are the core of bodhichitta practice, it is traditional and helpful to start with contemplations on equanimity and to conclude with sympathetic joy. Understanding the practices of equanimity and sympathetic joy greatly influences how the practices of loving kindness and compassion unfold.

THE PRELIMINARIES: COUNTING THE BREATH

Begin by taking a few minutes to center yourself and calm your mind. Sit comfortably in a quiet place. You can do this in your bedroom, in a shrine room, in a park, on an airplane, or on a mountainside—any place where you won't be disturbed for a short while.

Sit up straight and relax. Let your breathing slow down and become natural and full. To provide some structure to this preparatory phase, it is traditionally helpful to count your breaths. In and out is counted as one breath, and you can proceed by counting twenty-one breaths. If you lose track, don't worry. As soon as you come back, start counting again where you left off or last remember keeping count. Don't be hard on yourself if you wander off in your mind, but respect the moment when you notice this—which you naturally will—and then simply come back to counting your breaths. You can count one round of twenty-one breaths, or up to two or three rounds if you need more time to settle the energy in your body. Once you have completed one, two, or three rounds of twenty-one breaths, you will be quieter and calmer and ready to begin contemplating the four immeasurables.

EQUANIMITY

As I mentioned, we begin our practice of the four immeasurables with contemplations on equanimity. We will come back to the theme of equanimity throughout the other three immeasurable contemplations, but for equanimity specifically, we start by personally reflecting upon how, with every breath, we seek happiness. When we came into this world, we instinctually knew to turn toward our mother's breast to suckle and receive nourishment, warmth, and love. What is the origin of that primal knowledge, that urge to feed ourselves and to turn toward our mother as the source of our survival? We might say that this is biology or evolution or the instinct to survive, but where does that biology or instinct come from?

In all sentient beings there is an observable movement, drive, yearning, and wish for well-being and happiness. If you put a drop of water in front of an ant who's carrying a crumb back to his colony, he will pause and go around it, avoiding the potential obstacle to achieving his goal. Female mosquitoes seek blood to feed their eggs. What drives these urges? Of course, survival and procreation—but, once again, what is driving that?

What drives the female mosquito and the worker ant is an innate desire to flourish. We can say that flourishing and even procreation equate to some form of happiness. By happiness we do not necessarily mean "ha, ha, ha!" happy or an excited form of happiness. We are referring to *déwa*, or bliss, meaning physical and mental well-being and fulfillment.

This can take on many forms, but the experience is universal. We all equally recognize and appreciate the same inner experience of physical and mental well-being.

The stockbroker on Wall Street or the street food vendor in Varanasi ply their trades not necessarily because they love trading stocks or making *aloo-tikki*. They do what they do because it brings déwa, or happiness, on some level. It supports their family, feeds their children, allows for education, a home, vacations or breaks. All these things are equated to happiness or well-being. What drives us on a deeper level, more than mere evolution and procreation, is our wish for déwa, bliss, or happiness—in whatever form that may take for us individually. Granted, there are many ways in which beings seek happiness, including unhealthy and confused ways. The underlying drive for happiness is, nonetheless, the same. Ants and mosquitoes, cats and dogs, stockbrokers and street vendors, beggars and billionaires—all of us are exactly the same in striving, wishing, and working for happiness and doing our best to secure what we think will be the causes and conditions of our happiness.

Parallel to this, we all do our best to avoid any form of pain or suffering, along with what we think are the causes and conditions of pain and suffering. All beings possess an innate intelligence that knows the experiences of bliss and suffering, déwa and *dukkha*. This innate intelligence by nature moves toward happiness and pleasure and away from pain and suffering. We define a sentient being as one endowed with a mind that feels pain and pleasure, misery and happiness. Of course, we can only know our own experience. Everything else is based on inference. Rather than such inference being a problem, however, it greatly helps us in our practice of relative bodhichitta and the four immeasurables. Why so? Because, by taking our own personal experience as a base, we can then better understand others.

To put ourselves in another's shoes—human or otherwise—we must first understand what it is to be alive in our own. We have to be in touch with our own pain and suffering, our own happiness and joy. We must be in touch with our own innate drive to be happy and the parallel drive to avoid suffering in everything we do. Once we know this in ourselves, we can then explore how it is true for others.

We may look different from one another on the outside. We may have different skin colors and speak different languages, come from different cultures or races, have varying sexual or gender identities, belong to different religions and faiths, and have varying social values—and that is just in the human realm. We may have four legs or two legs, have horns growing from our head or antennae instead of eyes. We may live in the depths of the ocean or far beneath the surface of the earth. We may nest in trees, fly in the sky, or crawl on the ground.

In moving toward happiness and away from pain, however, we are all 100 percent equal. Just as we want comfort and well-being, so do others. Just as we wish to find success and fulfillment, to enjoy a good reputation and social acceptance, to be loved, appreciated, and acknowledged, so do others. Just as we wish to avoid any physical, mental, or emotional discomfort, to be spared the loss or destruction of what we love and value, and to be free from scorn, criticism, or insults, so do others. All beings, from top to bottom, are created equal in this way. Without exception.

The image for the practice of equanimity is an immense banquet held by a king for all his subjects, with each one served at the same table, regardless of social, economic, or any other differences. This is a helpful image to reference while contemplating equanimity.

LOVING KINDNESS

After spending a few minutes contemplating and acknowledging how all beings equally wish for happiness and freedom from suffering, we then move into the practice of loving kindness. Loving kindness, or the practice of *tséwa*, means generating tenderness toward all sentient beings, free from partiality. It is directed outward toward others but radically transforms our own mind and heart.

Once again, it is important to reflect on our constant yearning and working to obtain the causes and conditions of happiness, twenty-four hours a day, seven days a week. We wish for so many things: to have a good job, to save money, to overcome certain challenges, to progress on our path, to be kind toward others, to raise our children well, to not have a painful death, and so on. All these wishes arise from our innate yearning to be happy and to secure the causes and conditions of happiness. Just as we long for and work hard to obtain these various things, everyone else is doing the same.

Taking our own experience as a reference, we expand our mind and wish that all beings receive whatever they wish for, strive toward, and work on as a source of happiness. We unreservedly wish this for them. Initially, we start with those close to us in order to make our wish more personal and heartfelt. We can call to mind someone for whom love and affection easily arise. This can be a human being or a pet, someone alive or dead, or whoever inspires tenderness and the wish that they attain happiness and the causes and conditions of happiness, wherever they may be. We wholeheartedly wish for that individual to attain this—and even more so, that they attain the absolute wisdom of the nature of all things, which brings unconditional and absolute well-being, happiness, and bliss.

Once we genuinely feel this for someone we love, we then move outward. We wish that our family members and friends, coworkers and associates, neighbors and community members, wild and domestic animals, fish, birds, insects, and all living beings also attain whatever sources of happiness and well-being that they are working toward. May they attain this in full measure, with nothing lacking.

As an example, we might see a flock of geese flying south for the winter. We can take a moment and contemplate what this must be like for them. It is a long and arduous journey. They must navigate through bad weather, city lights, airplanes, and drones. They must find food and water, often traveling thousands of miles or more. We connect to them in our mind and wish that they attain whatever they desire, thinking, *May they make it safely to their destination, and may they succeed in raising their young to carry on the next generation.* We make our wish for beings' happiness quite specific and personal in this way and thus inspire our own creativity and exploration. We can freely connect to others and their striving for happiness, unreservedly wishing that all beings attain whatever it is they are seeking.

As a further layer to this practice, we want to call to mind all those we dislike, those who rub us the wrong way, those we disagree with, and even those who may possibly wish to harm us. We call them all to mind, one by one and together, sincerely contemplating what they must be working toward in their own lives and in their own ways.

This is possible because we generate tséwa based on the universal principle of equanimity. If we were to approach our practice of loving kindness from our self-centered emotional mindset, generating tenderness toward our adversaries would be extremely difficult. The self would not allow it.

When we come from a wisdom-oriented principle, which is based on the irrefutable, universal truth of equanimity, we can put aside our troubles and wish even our adversaries and enemies well. This is what makes the four immeasurables wisdom-based, rather than based on biology or our preferences. We can generate unconditional love for all beings equally because all beings equally wish for happiness.

This is how we put ourselves in others' shoes: just as we wish for happiness, freedom, and bliss and strive to secure the causes and conditions of our well-being and success, others share these same aspirations. Wishing this for ourselves alone or for a limited number of people close to us or on our side of the fence would, from the standpoint of the universal principle of equanimity, be unjust and nonsensical. Thus we wish for all beings to achieve, in full measure, whatever it is that they wish for.

We should not discount the various relative ways in which we and all sentient beings strive to be happy. These various forms of relative happiness have validity to a certain degree, but we don't stop there. Knowing that all relative things are compounded, impermanent, and at best able to provide only short-term fulfillment, we want to think, *In addition to attaining relative sources of happiness, may all beings, more importantly, attain the ultimate causes of happiness. May they be introduced to the wisdom of the Dharma and come to realize their own Buddha nature— the inherently awakened state of mind endowed with unconditional peace that all beings possess. May they diligently practice love and compassion on the bodhisattva path and attain complete liberation and freedom. May all beings become fully enlightened.*

Wishing from our heart that all beings attain both the relative and ultimate causes and conditions of happiness is the bodhichitta practice of loving kindness or tséwa. It is important to take it all the way from the relative to the absolute because true and lasting fulfillment, happiness, and peace are only found in realizing one's own nature and purifying all one's obscurations. Until that point, we continually strive in various ways to be happy on a relative level. Knowing this, we want to include in our bodhichitta practice both the relative forms of happiness and the ultimate, unconditional happiness of enlightenment.

Reciting this line from the four immeasurables prayer grounds us and helps us focus our mind: "May all beings have happiness and the causes and conditions of happiness. May all beings have happiness and the causes and conditions of happiness. May all beings have happiness and the causes and conditions of happiness."

The traditional image used for the practice of loving kindness is a mother bird tending her baby chicks. She tirelessly flies back and forth to the nest, tenderly feeding each of her young, cleaning out their waste, and making sure that they are safe and cozy until they are big enough to strike out on their own. Even then she stays close by to ensure that nothing happens to them. We can hold this image in our mind as we practice the immeasurable of loving kindness.

COMPASSION

After spending some time contemplating loving kindness, we then move into the immeasurable of compassion. In the practice of loving kindness, we focused on beings' happiness. In the practice of compassion, we contemplate beings' sufferings and cultivate a heartfelt wish that they may be free from suffering and the causes and conditions of suffering.

We begin again with a close and specific example. Think of a loved one who is going through a difficult time, or we can also think of ourselves if we happen to be facing some challenges. Patrul Rinpoche recommends imagining that we are a sheep about to be slaughtered by suffocation. He instructs us to put our hand over our mouth and nose and try to stop our breathing in order to feel a fraction of what it might be like to suffocate. He says to let ourselves feel some degree of the fear and panic of dying in this way and to imagine that we are, in fact, that sheep. The point of this contemplation is not to leave it in the abstract or just skim the surface.

We thus generate compassion for the suffering of those closest to us—a parent or someone who has cared for us deeply and is experiencing pain and suffering. It can be a beloved animal or anyone with whom there is no hindrance for empathy to arise. Experiencing empathy for those close to us makes us more familiar with the unencumbered feeling of compassion. We can then hold that quality of compassion as a reference point as we expand our compassion and empathy outward to others.

We can think of the suffering of those in our extended family, communities, or of animals and other innocent creatures. We then step out a bit further to those in our city or town and surrounding area. We keep extending further outward to include our whole country, and then think of various parts of the world—places we have been and those we have read about or seen in the news or on maps. Throughout the far reaches of our planet, in the depths of the oceans, lakes and rivers, in the mountains and the sky, underground and on the surface of the earth, there are countless beings—humans of all races, animals of all kinds, countless warm- and cold-blooded creatures. All of them wish to avoid any kind of suffering or pain, any threat to their existence. We want to reflect on how this is true for ourselves and understand how this is true for all beings.

Despite this wish that we all share, we nonetheless all experience a great deal of suffering and pain. From war, famine, disease, family disputes, abuse, neglect, addiction, violent crimes, hunger and thirst, internal tension and anxiety, physical and mental illnesses, and even the seemingly simple cycle of life—in all of this, beings go through tremendous and unimaginable suffering and pain. We want to call this to mind and sincerely wish that all beings be free from suffering and its causes and conditions. We can recite the four immeasurables prayer for compassion: "May all beings be free from suffering and the causes and conditions of suffering. May all beings be free from suffering and the causes and conditions of suffering. May all beings be free from suffering and the causes and conditions of suffering."

In particular, we want to bring to mind those whom we dislike, disagree with, feel a grudge toward, and even those who may have harmed us or others. This might be challenging in the beginning, but remember, this practice is based on principle—the wisdom-based universal principle of equanimity. This wisdom-based exercise of our heart builds strength and courage. Ultimately, we don't want to leave out anyone, because all beings without exception seek happiness and well-being and work to avoid anything physically, emotionally, or mentally painful. It is thus from a place of genuine equanimity that we generate compassion.

The traditional image for generating the bodhisattva's compassion is a mother who has no arms, watching as her only child is swept away by the powerful current of a river. Because she is armless, even if she were to jump in the river, she could do nothing to save her child. Nonetheless, she runs along the riverbank calling out, desperately wishing there were something she could do.

This powerful image might surprise us. The mother is helpless and yet feels so much. She would do anything to save her child, yet there is nothing she can do. Much of the time, what we think of as compassion and empathy is wrapped up with trying to fix a situation. If we look closely, we rarely allow ourselves to feel the raw, almost unbearable emotion of compassion without attempting to *do* something. This is natural on many levels, but if we examine it more deeply, we will likely notice that our urge to fix it, or "make it better," is often motivated by our own discomfort at witnessing another's suffering. Rather than genuinely attempting to put ourselves in the other being's position, feel what they are going through, and openly explore what they may need, we skip over this part and simply try to fix the situation. This shows us that our compassion, though well-intentioned, can tend to be more about ourselves than about others.

It takes courage and clarity to feel genuine compassion and empathy for others. It is not comfortable. It takes fortitude and an open heart to feel helpless yet stay there for another being who is in pain or struggling. Genuine compassion also requires wisdom to guide our actions—not just throwing fixes at things but being present in order to understand what is truly needed or to find out what really helps.

Part of this wisdom is acknowledging that beings have their own karma and their own minds, which are the root or source of what they are experiencing. Thinking that we can come in like an all-powerful being and change things for others is arrogant, foolish, and shortsighted. We may feel moved to act—and action can, of course, be good—but we must first be there to truly feel, like the mother without arms, with a courageous, brave heart that is present with the suffering of beings. Not only does this expand and strengthen our own mind and heart, but it provides a more accurate perspective on what may or may not be effective.

Many times there is nothing we can actually do, whether physically or verbally, to help another being in pain. But we can certainly open our heart and deeply feel what it must be like, without shutting down, becoming judgmental, or trying to fix. This can help more than we may initially realize. Exercising one's heart in this way makes an aspiring bodhisattva courageous and open, ready to act when there is, in fact, something available to do. When we feel helpless, when there is nothing we can offer to help another, many of us feel inclined to turn away—the discomfort of staying with the situation seems unbearable. Or we may feel that, since there is nothing we can actually do, it is pointless to stay there with it. But remaining open, keeping the person or the situation in our mind and heart and doing prayers that the situation may shift or resolve or find a way forward, this should not be discounted.

We might wonder what prayers and good wishes do to help. Such things may not seem tangible or effective in the moment, like putting out a fire with water. But staying soft and spacious and making aspirations that a difficult, stuck, or dire situation may change expands our own heart and makes us braver, more compassionate, accommodating, and tolerant toward others. This is precisely the strength and perspective needed to assess and discern whether there is something we can physically do. We might be surprised to find that our positive prayers and aspirations can subtly shift and affect situations, without our having to push our agendas onto others. Furthermore, making prayers and aspirations brings out our own inner qualities, preparing us to act, on the spot, with clarity, selflessness, and resolve.

Exercising and exploring our heart in this way gives the aspiring bodhisattva fortitude—the strength and ability to carry on and not easily burn out. After all, helping beings is not a short-term plan or a one-shot occurrence on the bodhisattva path. Aspiring bodhisattvas are in it for the long haul. If we truly want to walk the bodhisattva path and benefit beings, we must be willing to stay with others' suffering and let our heart expand and strengthen in this way. We must explore what it is to feel helpless, and yet still make sincere, heartfelt prayers that all beings be free from suffering and the causes and conditions of suffering. This is a powerful positive force to put out into the world.

Once, a student of mine accidentally ran over a rabbit while on the way to see me. They arrived distraught and in tears. Of course, it was terrible, and the person's pain was real. Their lamenting, however, was doing nothing to help the rabbit, which had just lost its life, nor was it helping their own state of mind. I suggested that they might put all that they were feeling into making sincere prayers for the rabbit. That they could dedicate all their own merit and virtue so that the rabbit might have a better rebirth and to focus their mind and heart in this way as a means not only to work with their own distress but to bring some measure of positivity to the being who had just died.

To make that kind of a connection to another being, to sincerely pray for their liberation, is powerful and beneficial. It is no longer about you; it is about the other. Not only does this approach make us stronger, it can truly help others. Going in this direction is a mind training, or lojong, which tangibly makes us braver, more openhearted, and ready to be there for others without becoming overwhelmed or tiring too quickly.

The Meaning of Practice

We want to give ourselves time on our meditation cushion to explore the practices of loving kindness and compassion, starting small, close, and specific, and then gradually expanding outward to include all beings throughout time and space. As beings are limitless in number, our love and compassion can likewise grow without limit. Like the rising sun first hitting the mountain peaks and then slowly spreading to fill every nook and cranny of the valleys below, our love and compassion can likewise spread to touch and include all sentient beings. This is why these practices are called immeasurables—as beings are immeasurable, there is no limit to the love and compassion that we can generate toward them. In time we can adopt all sentient beings into our love and compassion without hesitation or reserve.

Whenever we discuss the four immeasurables, the question about being a "doormat" arises. How can we know that we are not going to be taken advantage of or that others won't abuse our good heart? For many, this is a very valid concern, especially if a person is in a codependent, abusive, or unhealthy relationship. These are legitimate worries and should not be ignored. Sometimes we have to keep some physical and emotional distance in order to center ourselves and stay strong.

It is important to remember that the four immeasurables are an inner practice, done first and foremost on our cushion. We do not immediately jump up to save people, try to change their lives, or become a martyr. We must respect that beings have their own mind and karma and that sometimes it is not at all appropriate or even possible to do something to help others. At the same time, we can still work on our inner practice on the cushion in the safety and privacy of our own practice mind. After all, it is our inner practice that gives us the clarity, strength, and ability to assess how best to interact with others. Of course, we don't always get it right. This is a *practice*, which means we keep coming back; we keep learning. We fall down, but we get back up, and each time we gain greater perspective and strength.

The cushion is also where we can examine what happened and why. We can take time to review situations in our mind and gain clarity so that next time we can respond more effectively. It is helpful to remember that all neuroses are universal—there is nothing new or original in our own or anyone else's destructive thought patterns or afflicting emotions. All of these are based on habitual patterns in the mind.

As we discussed earlier, all habits are constructed. As they are constructed, they can also be deconstructed using the opposite of the four factors that create habits: repetition, intensity of action, lack of a counteragent, and the availability of the field. When we notice after the fact that we have been caught in our habitual reactive mind or a neurosis, we can sit down quietly and run through what happened from beginning to end, repeatedly if necessary. We can review how it all unfolded—where we lost our mindfulness and started to react habitually. Examining a past situation in this way gives us valuable information. This is how we come to see precisely where we need to be more vigilant and mindful, particularly regarding the four factors that construct and deconstruct habits.

Generally speaking, to avoid bigger upsets, we have to learn how to avoid the smaller upsets. Unless we learn how to apply patience to the small things that irritate or agitate us, expecting to apply patience toward a major irritant is too much to ask of ourselves. The habit has to build in increments, using the four factors that construct habits. We do this with small things, the little irritants, because these are not so heavy or difficult to work with. With these, we can more easily choose to be patient, to act differently, and to have more mindfulness. As we choose to work with our mind in a positive direction, those actions add up and take root, and we become more equipped to face bigger things. So we want to develop our awareness—in conversations, for instance, we can notice our choice to become riled and upset or to apply patience, to become reactive or to let go, to blurt things out or to remain silent and work internally with our reaction. This is how we build our strength to resist being so easily sucked in or upset, especially when bigger things happen.

Once again, this is the meaning of practice. We apply ourselves in small ways and slowly build our strength, clarity, and momentum. We are not expected to get it right from the get-go.

SYMPATHETIC JOY

Sympathetic joy is the fourth immeasurable; it is the practice of rejoicing. In the course of practice, we do this last because it elevates and seals the other three immeasurables. We start by thinking of someone for whom we easily feel happy. It could be a child, a parent, or a pet—or we can think of someone we admire and greatly appreciate, such as

Martin Luther King Jr., Mother Teresa, Helen Keller, Jesus, or Shakyamuni Buddha. It does not matter who it is, as long as we can immediately access the feeling of rejoicing in another person's life, deeds, and accomplishments.

Let's take the Buddha as an example. We can contemplate his life, how he was raised in luxury to become a king, but upon encountering the sufferings of old age, sickness, and death, he renounced his worldly destiny and went in search of the truth and how he might alleviate the suffering of beings. He spent six years in the most austere asceticism before realizing, at the point of almost dying, that he must tread the Middle Way. He accepted nourishment and took his seat under the bodhi tree near the Niranjana River in Bodh Gaya. He faced all the impediments to awakening—the *maras* of seduction and aggression—before coming to fully realize his own nature and attaining complete enlightenment.

Unsure if others would be able to understand the subtlety of his realization of the profound view of emptiness and dependent origination, he stayed silent in meditation for some time. Entreated to teach by countless celestial beings, including Brahma and Indra, who could see that he had realized the truth of all things, he finally found a way to communicate his realization to others. Thus began the Turning of the Wheel of Dharma, which has liberated countless beings. We, too, are the fortunate recipients of the Buddha's realization of the nature of all phenomena 2,600 years ago.

In pondering this, deep wonder and joy naturally arise for the deeds of the Buddha—for his sacrifice and his quest, for his perseverance and diligence, for his realization, and for his compassion in showing the path to others. We want to allow a deep sense of joyful wonder to swell within our heart, contemplating where humanity would be without the Buddha. The world is already an ocean of suffering. Where would we be if the Buddha's wisdom and compassion had not come about? Imagine humanity, and especially ourselves, without the Buddhadharma.

Genuine awe and sympathetic joy in the Buddha's life and deeds inevitably arise from such contemplations. We want to make a mental note of this unhindered feeling of rejoicing or sympathetic joy and hold that as a reference point as we continue our contemplations.

Once again, we call to mind someone close to us, someone for whom we feel a great deal of tenderness. Imagine them accomplishing all that they are working toward in whatever field it may be. Imagine them attaining their heart's desire. The same joy that we experienced while thinking of the Buddha's accomplishments, we can now engender while imagining our loved one succeeding. We want to wish them success in all their endeavors and also rejoice in deeds that they have already accomplished.

Once we genuinely feel that joy inside for our loved one's accomplishments, we can begin to reach out, thinking of others we care about. We want to take time to ponder what each one may be working on in their lives and sincerely wish them success. We can call to mind all of their accomplishments and rejoice in their successes as if they were our own.

Expanding out further, we include our extended family members, both those who are still alive and those who have long since passed away. We can rejoice on behalf of our community members, those living nearby in our city or town, in our state or province, in our country, and on our continent. Eventually, we rejoice on behalf of all living beings on this earth and beyond.

All beings are striving, working hard to secure happiness and its causes and conditions while avoiding pain and its causes and conditions. When someone is able to succeed and accomplish what they are working toward, how can we not rejoice? Especially if we are on the bodhisattva path—aspiring and working to attain enlightenment for the benefit of all sentient beings—whenever we encounter or imagine the success of anyone, we want to learn to sincerely rejoice on their behalf.

Particularly when we encounter someone who evokes jealousy or feelings of competitiveness, even subtly, we must work extra hard to wish them well and rejoice in even the smallest of their accomplishments. Sympathetic joy is a powerful tool for working with and overcoming jealous mindsets. Furthermore, we can think of those who harm beings and wish that they, too, may turn their minds toward altruism and virtue and make prayers of dedication that this may come to pass.

The traditional image for sympathetic joy is of a mother camel who has lost her baby and by chance finds him again. Mother camels are among the tenderest of mothers. They express deep unrelenting grief when something happens to one of their offspring. Should the baby camel be recovered, their mother's joy knows no bounds. This kind of joy is our model or image for the practice of sympathetic joy.

Sympathetic joy is unique in that it seals the rest of the four immeasurables. It does this because it thoroughly cleans out our heart, uncovering all our encrusted grudges, resentments, and competitive mindsets that can hide out even while we are practicing equanimity, loving kindness, and compassion. It brings to the surface any lurking self-centered neurosis that might arise and sabotage the best of our intentions. We must therefore not overlook or underestimate the profound and healing practice of sympathetic joy.

The four immeasurables are invaluable tools that we can use to soften our heart and awaken our mind every single day. When we talk about the practice of joyful exertion or diligence, it is in the context of what brings us lasting fulfillment, peace, and joy. Contemplating the four immeasurables and developing the brave heart of bodhichitta are precisely how we find such meaning. These practices bring us to the core of what it means to be alive as a fellow sentient being in this world and how we can make the most of our time here.

Speaking about diligence in this context is about giving ourselves the time and space to contemplate the teachings on the four immeasurables. It is about how to confront and overcome our layers of laziness that can hold us back and how to do all of this with joy and a bigger vision. We do not have to be Buddhist to contemplate and practice the four immeasurables. The only requirement is an open and curious mind and the wish to lead a meaningful life that is of benefit to oneself and others.

The approach of bodhichitta opens our eyes to an alternative way of life that benefits both others and ourselves. Adopting the way of the bodhisattva is a process that takes time. We can't expect to have the strength and knowledge of a great, altruistic being from the start. But something rings true for us in this approach. Perhaps we have already experienced the benefit of practicing the four immeasurables. Here we have an age-old, well-rehearsed, and mutually beneficial alternative to the rat race of our conventional world. Seeing this as our ticket to freedom and the very means of our own peace and happiness, we develop more conviction that this path of the buddhas and bodhisattvas is our own path. As our life experience unfolds and we are able to integrate the teachings of the four immeasurables into our day-to-day practice and interactions, our conviction blossoms into a joyful determination to deepen our practice of the way of the bodhisattva.

If we can take just twenty or thirty minutes each day and apply our mind to the contemplations of the four immeasurables, we will see and feel a change in our mind and heart, guaranteed. The more personal and self-reflective we can be in our contemplation and practice time, not merely saying or thinking things repetitively or ritualistically, the more positive change we will observe.

To make the four immeasurables a daily practice, we can memorize this short, yet complete prayer and recite it over and over whenever we wish—during formal practice on our cushion or at any time day or night. We can also say one of the lines, and then pause to contemplate that particular immeasurable before moving on to do the same with the other lines of the prayer.

> May all sentient beings enjoy happiness and the root of happiness.
> May they be free from suffering and the root of suffering.
> May they not be separated from the great happiness devoid of suffering.
> May they dwell in the great equanimity free from passion, aggression, and prejudice.

7

IGNORANCE IS *NOT* BLISS

6

All the paths of flight are blocked,
The Lord of Death now has you in his sights.
How can you take such pleasure in your food,
And how can you delight to rest and sleep?

One of our biggest internal impediments or sources of laziness is thinking that we will be here forever. We are all lulled by our ignorance and avoidance of impermanence. Shantideva is brutally honest here. The verses in this text are, in fact, his own words to himself. He is sharing them with those who also wish to reckon with their own frivolous, distracted mindsets. As we begin to recognize any or all of the three categories of laziness in ourselves, we might feel a surge of disbelief or amazement that we have been operating like this for so long. At the same time, we are filled with relief to finally see this part of ourselves clearly. As we wake up from our ignorance and denial, we are simultaneously inspired to make our lives meaningful and not to waste the precious time we have left. This transition from laziness to diligence, or from ignorance to wakefulness, only happens if we are willing to self-reflect and speak honestly and rigorously to ourselves, just as Shantideva speaks to himself.

We are all in samsara right now. We may not realize it yet, but we are like a fish caught in the fisherman's net. Like a fish about to be pulled up onto the deck of a boat, we are being drawn into the dire circumstances of old age, sickness, and death, and from there we do not know where we will take our next rebirth. It could be anywhere. We may find ourselves in worse conditions than now, like in the animal realm, or in a place that is consumed by floods, fires, famine, or war. We must ask ourselves, *What am I doing? Why am I wasting so much of my time in distraction, in dudzi? How can I continue sleepwalking through my life, assuming that these good conditions will last? Isn't this the time to act, when I still have agency and choice, when I am able to do something positive and meaningful? If I can't manage to do this now, when everything is in a good place, when will I get to what is most meaningful, to what I really want to do with my life?*

We can continue, saying, *Yesterday I was young, today I am old, and tomorrow I will die. Life goes by very quickly. I have friends who passed away at my age and even much younger, and I can't say where they have gone or where they are now. Even if I don't die today, I could die tomorrow. There is no guarantee that I will live to see the end of the week—and then what? So why am I wasting my time, distracted with frivolous pursuits and passions, taking on various extracurricular activities? Aren't I just like an animal who has no idea what to do, even while watching fellow animals being slaughtered one by one in front of me? How am I any different, just munching on my food and distracting myself with shortsighted "pleasures," not at all concerned about my own future or impending death?*

We don't want to take life for granted. These poignant thoughts and this straightforward self-talk about death give us a mental pinch to keep us from proceeding on autopilot. In many ways, life is like going through a passage. At the end of this passage, no one escapes slaughter. We all have to go through this passage, without exception. Everyone who was ever born dies. No one lives forever. All those who were alive 120 years ago are no longer here, and those who are here now will all be gone in another 120 years. We *all* die. That is the plain truth. So while we have the freedoms and advantages of this precious human birth, we need to practice bodhichitta and inspire ourselves toward virtue, altruism, and a meaningful life. We don't want to leave this life with nothing to show for it. Being praised by the world, leaving behind a famous legacy, or being judged well in the eyes of others—these things do absolutely nothing for us. We must make our life meaningful for ourselves, for our own journey forward, for our own satisfaction, fulfillment, and joy. We are the only ones who can live our own life and experience our own mind. Only we can shape this good heart of ours with the conditions we have at hand so that we can face the next phase with confidence and ease.

7

Death will swoop on you so swiftly.
Gather merit till that moment comes!
For even if you then throw off your indolence,
What will you do when there is no more time?

8

"This I have not done, and this I'm only starting.
And this—I'm only halfway through . . ."
Then is the sudden coming of the Lord of Death,
And oh, the thought "Alas, I'm finished!"

9

You'll look upon the faces of your hopeless friends,
Their tearstained cheeks, their red and swollen eyes
(For such will be the depths of their distress),
And then you'll see the heralds of the Deadly Lord.

10

The memory of former sins will torture you,
The screams and din of hell break on your ears.
With very terror you will foul yourself.
What will you do in such delirium?

As death approaches, many people can become filled with tremendous, overwhelming anxiety and fear. This is especially true for those who have led unvirtuous or extremely self-centered lives and deny any consequences of their actions. At the time of death, such people often have agonizing regret about how they have lived and can suffer greatly, antic-ipating the repercussions that may lie ahead. It can also be devastating for us to part with our loved ones and all that is familiar and terrify-ing to face the great unknown. Thus we must look honestly at the deep shenpa we have with our distractions and ask ourselves, *How long can I go on like this, distracted and caught up, when any day now I must sur-render to the Lord of Death, willingly or unwillingly?* Shantideva reminds us that it is a little too late to start thinking about how we might gain freedom when we are already lying on our deathbed. At that point, the body is too weak, and the mind is too fatigued and confused. We are halfway in this world and halfway in the next.

We are all vulnerable to suffering and loss in this life. However healthy and robust we may be—six-foot-four, with pumped muscles, looking like a statue of a Greek god—if we come down with a bad flu, we are just like a little bird who has been hit by a stone. We come crash-ing down onto our bed, losing all our energy, and curling up into the fetal position with the covers pulled over our head. There is nothing permanent in our physique, strength, health, wealth, or power. When we are struck by serious illness, we are like a fish dropped on dry sand: writhing, helpless, and completely vulnerable.

When we are ill, even seriously ill, we still have our physical body to ground our mind in this world. In the intermediate stage between this life and the next (*bardo*), however, we have no physical form. For a period of time, we have only a light body. It might sound nice to have a body made of light, but it is not a pleasant experience. The instability of bardo beings is said to be seven times more out of control than a diagnosed schizophrenic. After we leave the bardo and take rebirth in our next life, we could again end up vulnerable, at the mercy of our own negative karma or deeds, like a lobster or crab about to be boiled alive in a Chinese or French restaurant, our flesh cooked up for others to enjoy. What can a lobster or crab do in that situation other than suffer in pain, totally helpless and vulnerable? Before we get to that point, before it is too late, we must aspire to bodhichitta and the practice of altruism and the four immeasurables. We must appreciate and value the practice of virtue and learn to exert ourselves with joy.

11

If, like a living fish that twists and writhes,
You are so terrified while still alive,
What need to speak of pain unbearable
In hells created by past evil deeds?

12

How can you remain at ease like this
When you have done the deeds that lead
To contact on your tender baby-flesh
Of boiling liquids in the hell of Extreme Heat?

The teachings say that hell realm beings have extremely soft, sensitive, baby-like skin. Those of us who are always trying to keep our skin young and supple, using products and procedures to make it look smoother, softer, and moister, may find it curious to learn that hell realm beings have just such skin. Hearing this, we might feel a bit envious of the suppleness of their skin, but for them having such fine skin is a disadvantage. It makes their suffering that much more intense. It is ironic that what the multibillion-dollar cosmetics industry is trying to peddle to us makes hell realm beings' pain so much more acute.

13

So testy and thin-skinned, you want results without endeavor—
Many are the troubles now in store for you!
Though in the grip of death, you are behaving like a god,
And suffering, alas, will beat you down!

Shantideva is speaking to us, helping us to peel back the layers of our laziness and our conditional, temporary indifference for our own benefit. In this case, he is pointing out that, when we default to a place of self-absorbed emotional sensitivity—being easily offended, for instance, assuming that everything anyone says is directed against us—this is, from the Buddhist teachings point of view, a form of laziness. We are lazy about taking responsibility for our own mind and emotions.

Ultimately, we don't want to be accountable for our actions or reactions. This makes it hard for us to ever find peace or joy. And if we dig in our heels, justifying our reactions and defending them to the death, we will be engulfed by suffering guaranteed. In this state of mind, our tolerance for the world and others, especially those closest to us, wears thinner and thinner, like a blister ready to burst, revealing red raw flesh underneath.

It is not that more is happening to us than to others. Everyone is living their lives and working through whatever is arising for them. When we become testy and thin-skinned, however, we tend to feel particularly offended by things, as if the world has turned against us, singled us out, or is targeting us. This is called *nangwa dra lang* in Tibetan, meaning "all appearance arises as an enemy." Whenever we become overly sensitive like this, we also find suffering.

This kind of touchy, sensitive state of mind generally arises from an overindulgence in our preferences or shenpa. We have overindulged in clinging to how we want things to be, rather than working with how things really are. Our indulgence assumes a kind of privileged stance, as if we have the exclusive right to be sensitive, to hold on to our preferences, and to demand that others abide. In fact, we have become spoiled—spoiled by our own selves.

In these verses, Shantideva's self-talk is like chastening a spoiled child. Here the spoiled child is our ego—the self-centered, self-absorbed mindset. These verses are the self-talk of a bodhisattva who wishes to "grow up" and make genuine progress on the path and in their own life for the benefit of beings. We realize that we lack diligence, but due to our positive motivation and good intentions, we also want to exert ourselves in a sustainable way. We want to wake ourselves from the slumber of samsara. This slumber, as lulling as it can be at times, is like that of an animal sleeping outside the butcher's door. So we encourage ourselves, remembering how short life is, how sure death is to come, and how delusional it is to think that we have all the time in the world to do everything we may wish to do.

Shantideva asks us to open our eyes, look around, and acknowledge what we see. Some people die just as they are starting a family, some as a young child or an infant, some when they are middle-aged, and some when their children are grown and they are very old themselves. There is absolutely no certainty about when or how we will die. It could be sudden and unexpected or long and drawn out—and at the beginning, middle, or end of our potential life span.

When impermanence stares us in the face, however attached we are to this life and to our family and friends, however much we don't want to die or our friends and family don't want us to die, once the time comes we have no choice. We must go forward naked and alone. What will help us most at this time is the Dharma and our practice of altruism. This and our bank of virtuous deeds are what give us strength, clarity, and confidence to face our inevitable transition with some measure of grace and ease.

The good news is that right now it is not too late. Right now we have the time, the liberty, and the opportunity to take ourselves in hand and do something that will help us, both in the present and at that crucial moment. We don't want to obsess over our impending death merely for the sake of instilling fear—what would be the point of that? The point of keeping death in the forefront of our mind is to live a more meaningful life and to prepare ourselves to face this transition with confidence and ease.

14
So take advantage of this human boat.
Free yourself from sorrow's mighty stream!
This vessel will be later hard to find.
The time that you have now, you fool, is not for sleep!

Some of us—and perhaps all of us to a certain degree—think that the point of life is to seek and maintain pleasure and happiness through external, material activities and things. We rarely pay attention to our mind and the role it plays in the experience of genuine happiness and contentment. How often do we reflect that the mind is the experiencer of all happiness and all suffering? How often do we explore how happiness, freedom, fulfillment, and joy can be cultivated and suffering overcome through our inner discipline on the spiritual path—such as pursuing the practice of the four immeasurables with joyful exertion? How many of us realize the opportunity that our precious human life—so hard to gain and so easy to lose—grants us to overcome the deep habitual sleep of ignorance? Most of us do not realize that the opportunity of having a human body can be used either as a boat to cross over the ocean of samsara or as the very thing that will pull us down into the depths of misery, pain, and suffering.

Without realizing it, we often become irritated or angry with those who support and love us the most—our parents, friends, teachers, and family members. How many times in this last week alone have we reacted toward others with aggression and rejection or turned that aggression upon ourselves? Instances like this don't just fade away without repercussion or consequence. Such angry outbursts, seething resentments, or subtle aggression—directed toward ourselves or others—can sow seeds in our mind stream and easily forge themselves into habits as we continually indulge in them. When the right causes and conditions come together, those seeds and the force of the habit are right there, ready to emerge with greater strength than before. How can we sit idly back, not relating to any of this and pretending that there are no seeds to ripen, no consequences to our actions, or that we are not indulging in reinforcing our habits of aggression and attachment?

Shantideva exhorts us not to sleepwalk through life in a state of ignorance but to think and talk to ourselves, to actively remind ourselves of what is at stake, and to not take our positive conditions for granted. It is in this context that we emphasize the immediacy of practice and of joyfully applying and exerting ourselves every single day toward leading a meaningful life.

This concludes the section of the text that cultivates awareness of the laziness of yearning for idleness and sleep.

Verse 15, which we begin to explore here, and verse 16, which will come several chapters later, are about cultivating awareness of the laziness of distracting preoccupations and unwholesome actions.

15

You turn your back upon the Sacred Doctrine,
Supreme joy and boundless source of bliss.
Why delight in mere excitement,
In distractions that will cause you misery?

For the most part, how we experience the world, other beings, and even our own mind comes down to how we orient ourselves. This orientation arises from a deeper level of motivation. Samsara is built on looking outward and grasping for things with which to cherish the self. We then try to capture those things, while pushing away anything that gets in our way. We generally orient ourselves from this place of attachment to the self, and that is the foundation of the conventional mindset. The baseline position of self-centered attachment seeks fulfillment for the self above all else, while the perspective of altruism seeks happiness and peace equally for all beings. These are two very different baselines, orientations, and motivations. Here, Shantideva urges us to objectively examine what brings genuine, reliable happiness, freedom, and peace and where the so-called pleasures of samsara lead.

8

EMBRACING THE UNIVERSAL SELF

Throughout Shantideva's text, we are challenged to reflect on how we relate to our body and to our life because this is where our self-centered orientation manifests most. We generally take our attachment to our body as a given. We consider our body as the basis for our existence, and it is therefore our primary reference point. Because we are so dearly attached to our body, we unconsciously assume that our body and the whole of our existence are one and the same. Of course, they are related and presently intertwined, but this unconscious misperception, or exaggeration, makes us cling unnecessarily tightly to our body. Based on this clinging, we work hard to cherish and secure the body's health, youth, beauty, well-being, longevity, and so on. Many of our self-centered emotions and neurotic activities flow from these efforts—from trying to cherish and protect our body, which we erroneously assume is the basis for all that we experience. It is not that the body is unimportant, but the extreme clinging that manifests in relation to our attachment to the body can cause us a great deal of confusion and strife.

In the Dharma, we acknowledge that we have this amazing body and that we certainly do experience many things through our body at this time. Thus we naturally want to use it well and to the best of our ability as a vessel to cross the ocean of samsara, particularly while we still have favorable conditions. Ultimately, there is no guarantee that we will find these conditions in the future, either in this life or the next. Things change all the time. So what do we do instead of cherishing the singular self that we assume to reside in our body? What do we do with all the attachment that we have to both our body and this small self? The Dharma introduces us to the possibility of thinking bigger. It reveals our potential to embrace a larger "universal self." This universal self includes ourselves as we are, but it also equally includes all sentient beings without exception.

Generally speaking, our clinging to the small self and our body comes from a certain warmth that we have toward ourselves. People who have an ordinary, healthy sense of self feel naturally warm and tender toward themselves. This is present in all that they do to meet their needs and take care of themselves. In the Buddhist teachings, this sense of self is still the ego, still the small self, and still based on ignorance, but it is a functional level of ego and self, rather than a self-absorbed, self-centered clinging to the self. This ordinary, functional healthy sense of self can, in fact, be useful in learning how to embrace the universal self. We can utilize the attentiveness that we have toward ourselves as a basis to expand upon and from which to adopt all beings as our universal self. Just as we care for all parts of our dear body and work to meet the countless needs and desires of the self, we can employ that same attention and consideration to cultivate universal love and care equally for all beings.

There is an important point that we should address at this juncture. In the West, I have observed an additional element when discussing using the ordinary healthy sense of self as a basis for embracing all sentient beings as part of our universal self. Many years ago, I mentioned to one of my great teachers, Trulshik Rinpoche, that there were people—particularly, though not exclusively, in the West—who didn't like themselves, were aggressive toward themselves, and even caused themselves harm. He could not understand how this could be so. In old cultures, not only in Asia, but also in Western countries several hundred years ago, the modern-day notion of self-hatred or self-loathing was not widespread. The tendency to be extremely hard on oneself, overly critical, or aggressive toward oneself can thus be difficult for older teachers (lamas) or those from more traditional cultures to understand. Of course, not all people experience or feel self-hatred or self-aggression. I have found that, overall, most people have a fairly sound and relatively healthy sense of self. Nonetheless, there are many who have experienced trauma in their lives, perhaps due to not having received genuine, wholesome warmth or love from their parents or parental figures as they were growing up, among other reasons. As a result, some people develop a negative view of themselves.

Those who suffer from self-hatred and self-loathing must find balanced ways to work with this and heal themselves, and I fully support them in this journey. Alongside this healing journey, it is also important to keep in mind that, just as pride and arrogance have an extra dose of self-clinging beyond what we might consider an ordinary, healthy sense of self, self-hatred is often the other side of that same coin. Knowing that extreme self-criticism and pride are both rooted in a heightened level of self-absorption can be liberating and can give us great hope for being able to let go.

Honestly reflecting on our self-absorption, without falling into either extreme of unworthiness or arrogance, opens up space in our mind to develop wholesome self-love. Cultivating wholesome self-love balances and remedies many of our more extreme tendencies. It grounds us and shows us the beauty of simply being ordinary—not the worst in the world or the best in the world. Maybe we do not have to fulfill all the expectations we or external conditions seemingly impose on us, nor come down hard on ourselves should we fail to achieve all these things. Maybe we don't have to be either the top dog or at the bottom of the food chain. Maybe we can simply be who we naturally are and learn to feel secure and have confidence in that. It is possible to accept ourselves—both flaws and strengths—and be OK with that. We could come back to the middle and be at ease with being neither the worst nor the best, but simply ordinary.

In that space, we can explore what it is to have an ordinary, healthy sense of self. There is room to develop warmth and kindness toward ourselves in a natural and grounded way. In that natural space of ordinariness, we also have room to develop ordinary self-care. Eating well, exercising, working to support our family, or any of the other ways in which we take care of our designated, functional self are not necessarily problematic for us. This functional self is not the self or ego that the Dharma points to as the source of all our suffering. The self becomes problematic when, for whatever reason, we develop a pattern of thinking only about ourselves, or "me and mine," and exclude anyone or anything that falls outside that designation. When absorbed in getting what we or what anyone whom we consider an extension of ourselves wants—especially when our self-absorption attempts to do this at the expense of others—that is when the self becomes a problem. That is the self that the Dharma points to as the source of all our suffering.

The self, therefore, becomes a problem when we are sensitive only to our own experiences of pain and pleasure and regard others' experiences with an attitude of "What? Who has pain besides me? Who has anything going on in their lives besides me?" In that mindset we are unaware of others, closed down inside our own self-absorbed cocoon.

As we learn to distinguish the problematic self from our functional, ordinary self and discover that we can let go of our self-importance and self-absorption, we need something to take its place. We need to fill the gap left behind as we let go. We fill this gap with universal love toward all beings who, just like us, are working day and night to find fulfillment, peace, and joy and to avoid any pain or suffering. In developing a universal self, we do not stop the flow of our love, care, and compassion directed toward ourselves; rather the object of that love and care changes and expands. We grow the small self into the universal self— which still includes ourselves, just not exclusively.

Lotuses do not blossom and flourish in dry ground; they need a muddy pond in which to bloom. With this image, the Buddha illustrates how bodhichitta does not grow in a passionless state. It grows where our passions—meaning our care, love, concern, and protectiveness—arise in regard to our small self. Our passions are like the mud. Learning that we can use this mud to grow and expand our sense of self to include all sentient beings and to embrace them all as our universal self with universal love or bodhichitta—that is the lotus. In this way our attachment to the self and our body can teach us a lot. Knowing how it feels to dearly cherish and look after the self and our body, we use that experience as a reference to then embrace all sentient beings, without exception, with the same feelings of love and compassion. This process naturally purifies the neurosis of the old small self without having to get rid of anything.

This is the practice—this is what we are learning to be diligent with. There are many steps to this, especially for those who have endured trauma, who are exceptionally hard on themselves, or who often feel that they are not good enough or not worthy—or, on the other hand, who are arrogant, prideful, and feel superior to others.

In our modern culture in both the East and the West, we find so many ways to compare ourselves with others—in movies, magazines, ads, social media, and on TV. These images all have an impact on us, whether or not we realize or like to admit it. Additionally, our schooling, testing, and the fostering of "good-natured competition" also impact us. Many people suffer greatly in our culture of comparison and competition. So we must first work on recovering our ordinary healthy sense of self, and then, without rejecting anything, work on developing our bodhichitta as an extension of the love and care that we already have for ourselves.

Learning to adopt all sentient beings as our "self" and to relate to the world through this perspective is the Dharmic approach. Thus we dedicate our body, speech, merit, and possessions to our adopted universal self—to all living beings. This is the spirit and the way of the bodhisattva. This is what Shantideva is challenging and urging us to grapple with and to realize as a possibility—for our own sake more than anything else.

Sometimes we may feel resistance to what the Dharma is teaching us. We may feel unsure about embracing what we are learning. The Dharma questions our singularly self-centered orientation, which we usually take for granted. This is our opportunity to ask ourselves: *What do we lose by studying and practicing the Dharma?* The Dharma is going to work against our habits and our habitual way of thinking, and it is going to come up against our assumptions and our attachments, so we should expect to feel challenged. But along with feeling challenged, we also want to frequently ask ourselves, *What do we* stand to lose in this, other than our ego attachment, which causes all our suffering?

At times we may feel that we are faced with a choice: to be open, trusting the wisdom of the Dharma, personally taking it to heart, and integrating it as a means to transform and awaken our greater potential, or to simply stay the way we are. This choice comes down to our interest. *Interest* is a small, common word, so we may not feel its impact right away. But it all comes down to how willing and interested we are to do the work of integrating the Dharma into our mind and life, not just for the sake of intellectual knowledge or fascination, but in order to truly let go of the very thing which, on the one hand, we are so attached to, but on the other causes all our pain. For many of us, it feels easier and more comfortable to simply carry on with our old patterns, thinking that nothing is wrong with that. After all, they are familiar and we know them so well.

We might also have the opinion that the Dharma is simply another form of dogma and that our resistance is therefore valid. Perhaps on one level the Dharma is a dogma, but we are always following one form of dogma or another. Any opinion opposing the Dharma is likely also based on dogma, perhaps the dogma of the ego itself or the dogma of our conventional world and its value system. We may think that we are coming from an objective point of view, and maybe we are, but our mind and our values are shaped by our culture, particularly by our modern-day conventional consensus and whatever subset of that consensus we are drawn to adopt. So the question to ask ourselves might be, *Which dogma has more wisdom and ultimately benefits myself and others the most—in the short and the long run?* Considering this openly and respectfully can calm any automatic rejection of what we are learning. This approach gives us room to contemplate and, if we so choose, to integrate these ideas, which may initially seem radical and challenging.

9

THE THREE WISDOMS

Hearing, Contemplation, and Meditation

Studying the Buddha's teachings and the wisdom of enlightened mind as expressed through either the spoken or the written word is a process of integrating the three wisdoms. We take in what we hear or read, ponder whether it is so, and consider how it relates to us and our inner life. This last part is crucial. We don't want to accept things at face value or make any assumptions. As the Buddha said, "Examine my words like a goldsmith examines gold. Don't take my words as truth simply because they come from me." We are thus heartily encouraged to personally contemplate what we learn from a teacher or the teachings. This is especially so on the Buddhist path, but the same principle can be applied to any form of wisdom that we encounter.

I would like to call our attention to a particular point in the Buddha's instructions, which we may easily overlook. To examine "like a goldsmith examines gold" implies an understanding of the knowledge, skill, and experience needed in the craft of goldsmithing. No one is born an expert goldsmith, immediately able to distinguish real from false gold. That skill must be developed gradually, over time, and requires dedication, patience, and experience. For us, this means being humble and open. We must take care not to assume that we know it all from the beginning.

The thing about genuine wisdom is that, once we hear it, we do not forget. It haunts us. It is important to respect this, but it is also important to be humbly honest about where we currently are. There is always progress to be made. That is why it is called *the path*. We are not meant to accomplish the fruition of the path when we are just starting out or when we are somewhere in the middle. This is why we continually cultivate our Dharma education through the three wisdoms of hearing, contemplation, and meditation.

The three wisdoms are how we integrate the Dharma into our lives, allowing for measured and stable progress on the path. Without the three wisdoms, we are bound to be quite lost when striving to adopt a universal self, for instance, in place of our small, singular self. After all, prior to first hearing the Dharma, our only other reference point was most likely conventional wisdom, which sees the world, first and foremost, through the lens of looking out for number one. In the beginning, personally embracing a larger perspective that, in fact, better serves our purpose can seem quite radical.

Once we begin to observe and personally experience the common sense and practical advantage offered by embracing the universal self, as an example, we don't want to stop there. Based on our experience and what we have heard, we inspire ourselves to further cultivate our contemplation and meditation. The three wisdoms work together, building upon one another. After hearing teachings about the universal self, and if they ring true for us, we then contemplate further by asking ourselves, *How do I work on changing my deeply embedded habit of orienting and assessing everything from the central headquarters of my self-cherishing mindset? How do I gain some space from "the self" itself?* Exploring this on our cushion is an example of exercising our contemplative wisdom.

Once we have exhausted that conceptual analysis for the time being, we can then rest in the wakeful, present nature of our mind, letting our thoughts arise and dissolve naturally without chasing after their content. When we meditate, we allow ourselves to open up in a nonconceptual way to the wisdom we have conceptually absorbed. Only then does that wisdom take root, penetrating and affecting the deeper layers of our ignorance. This is an example of meditative wisdom. We can alternate between conceptual analysis (contemplation) and nonconceptual resting (meditation) and thus naturally enhance the presence of the three wisdoms in our own day-to-day experience.

If you hear something in a teaching that resonates with you, take time to examine how and why that is so. Use the invaluable process of contemplative wisdom to gain clarity and confidence—not arrogance or pride—on that particular subject. If something does not resonate or you have questions about it, don't simply assume that you are already an expert and discount or reject what you are hearing. Stay open, keep asking, keep pondering, keep learning. Isn't that the attitude or sign of one who is truly learned and wise? The Buddha had no reason to lie to us about anything, so we can at least have that level of openness, curiosity, and respect toward his teachings.

Practicing the three wisdoms—hearing, contemplating, meditating—accumulates tremendous merit, or positive energy, and wisdom. This wisdom and merit are like our rudder, assuring that we sail straight and true in the vessel of our human body across the ocean of samsara and delusion, swiftly reaching the shore of liberation. Developing and engaging our wisdom and merit bring tremendous joy and meaning to our life. As we accumulate the three wisdoms, we begin to notice how painful our mindless distractions and laziness are. Scrolling, watching TV, sleeping in, and other "pleasures" of samsara waste our precious time and accomplish nothing more than letting our life slip through our fingers, day after day, year after year. Before we realize it, we are already bald and losing our teeth, hunched over and barely able to walk. We become less and less capable and gradually realize we are approaching our death.

Reminding ourselves of what we truly wish to accomplish in this life, what we must do with the limited time that we have left before it is over, and allowing such reflections to sink in and work on us—that is how we awaken our dull, listless mind. These contemplations spur us on and pinch us awake. Many great masters have said, "In the beginning, reflections on impermanence and death allow you to enter the path. In the middle, they urge you to strive diligently to accomplish what you want to achieve. And in the end, they become the deathless state of the dharmakaya itself." This is nothing other than a process of the three wisdoms, and this is the kind of straightforward self-talk, self-admonishment, and self-encouragement that Shantideva exhorts us to engage in. It is, in fact, the kindest thing we can do for ourselves— the best form of "self-care."

So let's try to do as Shantideva prescribes. Let's try to put our mind to work in search of understanding the things that don't yet make sense to us. Let's use this practical understanding to gain perspective regarding what we are doing and why we are doing it, whether in the Dharma or in our lives in general.

We all must assess how far we have come, how far we still have to go, and what we must do in order to get there. We all know that we can do better. We can all do a bit more to let go of our dudzi, our distracting preoccupations, our self-satisfaction, and our laziness that likes to give ourselves a pass. Time and again, we all must take a good look at ourselves, assess what is most meaningful, let go of what is not, then pull ourselves up by our bootstraps and get to it.

10

LEARNING TO PRIORITIZE AND APPRECIATING OUR HARDSHIPS

Whether we are talking about the spiritual path or conventional ambition, what allows us to overcome the obstacles to accomplishing what we wish to achieve is learning, and relearning, how to prioritize our "to-do lists." We have these lists in both our spiritual and conventional pursuits. To prioritize our to-do lists, we must think carefully about what we will gain by achieving what we set out to do and what we will lose by being carried away by distractions and wasting our time.

The spiritual path and conventional pursuits each have different foundations and different outcomes. One is limited to this life and is generally centered on the small self. The other is ideally centered on bodhichitta and embraces the universal self that strives for the benefit of all sentient beings. If we wish to have any measure of success in either approach, we must work to inspire ourselves on a daily basis, joyfully apply effort toward what we wish to engage and accomplish, and try to minimize and let go of our various distracting preoccupations and laziness. Even though the foundation and the outcome of a spiritual life and a conventional life differ greatly, the methods used to accomplish what we wish for are similar.

In both cases, it is helpful to be aware of our timetable. For example, in conventional life, we must get good grades in elementary and middle school or at least pass in order to enter high school. The same is true in high school so that we can enter college, especially the college of our choice. Then we must do well in college to have a chance at a good job and a promising career.

Similarly, we want to appreciate the timetable of our spiritual path. We don't want to take our present supportive conditions for granted, nor assume that we can skip ahead without carefully cultivating the essential, foundational aspects of our path. Acknowledging how learning to prioritize helps us progress now and in the future assists us in minimizing our distractions and joyfully engaging with our to-do lists.

Another measure that can help us prioritize our efforts and let go of distractions is developing a healthy appreciation for hardships, especially on the spiritual path. Sakya Pandita said in *Excellent Speech of Sakya*, "While training the mind, we are bound to face challenges. With too much leisure, we never achieve anything worthwhile. Difficulties and hardships force us to grow, allowing us to reap the fruit of that growth in our lives." That is why he also said, "In training, all great beings have gone through challenges. With this perspective, we must welcome challenges when they arise." This is the opposite of wanting to train our mind and have the fruition of that growth while also trying to maintain a life of distracted leisure, so to speak. Encountering hardships and challenges and then engaging in the process of facing and overcoming them—this is what produces accomplishment in any field.

It is not like hardships exist in one box and accomplishments in another. They are the same thing. The difference is in the outcome, which is shaped by how we engage and relate to what arises in our lives. Ask anyone who has faced challenges and come out the other side—this is where the most growth takes place. We must thus maintain this perspective and welcome what comes on the path, accepting any obstacle as good challenge, knowing that, without facing some hardship, accomplishment won't simply fall into our lap.

Learning to be inspired by challenges is a process itself. The mind needs shaping and direction; it needs training to value the growth that comes with seeing through the difficulties and impediments that inevitably arise on the path and in life. Without consciously choosing to face and be inspired by whatever challenges may arise for us, the mind won't be prepared or conditioned to know what to do when problems appear. Developing and reinforcing our conscious choice is a big part of mind training.

For example, we may be addicted to distractions or engulfed by laziness, but due to our hearing wisdom, we know what we have to do. We are inspired by the challenge to let go of our distracting preoccupations in order to make space for our greater goals. Excusing ourselves from this challenge and convincing ourselves that our distractions or our laziness have validity while also wanting to achieve greater meaning in life is, as the teachings say, like trying to ride two horses in opposite directions at the same time. It just doesn't work.

16

Do not be downcast, but marshal all your powers;
Make an effort; be the master of yourself!
Practice the equality of self and other;
Practice the exchange of self and other.

In essence, the Diligence Chapter comprises these four ideas:

1. Do not be downcast.
2. Marshal all your powers.
3. Make an effort.
4. Be the master of yourself.

At the beginning of the Diligence Chapter, Shantideva presented the obstacles, acknowledging where we are and introducing the three types of laziness. Once we are "inside," so to speak, he gives us tools to more thoroughly understand where we are and how to work with what is arising. These tools are the "four allies" and "two strengths." He shows us how to apply these tools so that we can become supple and proficient in what we wish to pursue, and thus we slowly learn how to become the master of ourselves. Doesn't this sound wonderful? Verse 16 outlines the message and the teachings of the entire Diligence Chapter. The points outlined here are, of course, extremely useful on the spiritual path, but they can be applied in any field at all.

We will go into greater detail of each of these four ideas as the chapter unfolds, but briefly, "do not be downcast" in Tibetan is *jéluk mépa*, which means being free from laziness or obstacles. Jéluk mépa literally means "without heaviness," or free from the heaviness of laziness. "Marshal all your powers" is *pungtsok* in Tibetan, which refers to gathering the four allies. *Pung* means force or power, and *tsok* means to gather. The two strengths are "make an effort" and "be the master of yourself," respectively, *lhur langwa* and *wangdu jawa* in Tibetan.

The first strength, lhur langwa or "make an effort," means to consistently apply effort or earnest application. This idea explores the use of *bakyö* and *shézhin*, mindfulness and vigilant introspection. Engaging these two aspects of our mind is precisely what allows our effort to be earnest. The second strength, wangdu jawa, literally means "exerting control," and refers to learning to be the master of oneself. It is not about tightly regulating something, however. Once we are aware of our challenges, are willing to work with them with confidence, and can rely on the tools of the four allies and two strengths, our joyful diligence and effort become second nature to us. At this point, we have such a thorough understanding of our mind and what we wish to do—knowing all the ins and outs of what might arise and how we will face those challenges with the tremendous wealth and tools of the Dharma—that we joyfully proceed and make progress as we wish. That is the meaning of wangdu jawa. This is how our diligence becomes second nature to us, and how we therefore become the master of ourselves.

This verse illustrates and summarizes how diligence is not magic but rather is discovered by being honest with ourselves, increasing our self-inspiration through facing our challenges and obstacles, employing the four allies, and continuously practicing mindfulness and vigilant introspection.

Shantideva provides this outline here so that we can begin to grasp the structure of his presentation. Up until now, the verses have explored where we currently stand. We now know the lay of the land. Here, he begins to present the tools, revealing how we can work with the obstacles and our laziness, overcome our dense mental fog, and attain our goal.

The Buddhadharma never leaves us stranded, wondering where to start or what to come back to. We always begin with turning our mind and interest toward developing bodhichitta, and we continually return to this as our base. Our diligence ultimately develops in relation to this. Bodhichitta is like a temple in our heart that is supported by four pillars—the four immeasurables. As we work on developing and strengthening these pillars, we also need a way to measure or evaluate how well we are doing, to self-assess and be sure that we are practicing properly in the way the teachings are intended to be practiced.

11

THE THREE MEASURES OF ASPIRATION BODHICHITTA

Equanimity, Exchange, and Considering Others as More Important than Oneself

Developing aspiration bodhichitta marks the true starting point of the bodhisattva path. Everything we work on as aspiring bodhisattvas, including practicing the four immeasurables, leads up to this moment: the genuine wish to attain enlightenment for the benefit of all beings. That singular intention is the seed of liberation.

We don't arrive at this point once and are then done with it; we cultivate this altruistic aspiration over and over again as part of our bodhichitta practice. This is a process, and we are meant to develop and go through changes as we move toward enlightenment. When cultivating our aspiration bodhichitta and altruism and growing our universal self, there are traditionally three measures or gauges with which we can assess our progress: equanimity, exchange, and considering others as more important than ourselves.

EQUANIMITY

The first of these measures or gauges is to notice how much we consider ourselves and others as equal—in wishing for happiness and in wanting to avoid suffering.

His Holiness the Dalai Lama often reminds us that engaging in the practices of equanimity, loving kindness, compassion, and sympathetic joy—the four immeasurables—as a means for achieving happiness and freedom for all beings naturally ensures our own well-being and peace of mind. Even conventionally speaking, how can we go wrong generating genuine, unconditional kindness and compassion toward others? How can we go wrong working on our patience and generosity toward others or being morally conscientious? How can we go wrong cultivating meditation and wisdom and living a life dedicated to the welfare of others? And how can we go wrong working on our diligence, which supports all of these?

We want to continually reflect and remind ourselves that considering others as equal to ourselves is acknowledging that all beings want to be happy and free from suffering in exactly the same manner as we wish for these things. There is absolutely no difference between us and others in this regard. Despite our varying outer conditions, whatever those may be—cultural, social, generational, ethnic, gender-based, or any other differences that we can imagine—the fact remains that all beings strive toward happiness and move away from pain with every breath they take. If we consciously acknowledge this, it is almost impossible to sacrifice others' well-being for our own gain. As this acknowledgment sinks in deeper, we come to a point where we would gladly sacrifice our own comfort for the sake of others. In the past, we have without a second thought sacrificed others' well-being for the sake of our own happiness or gain. This has only dug us deeper into our own pit of suffering, confusion, and pain. Now that we have heard the wisdom of the Buddha, are contemplating what we have heard, and are beginning to bring it into our meditation in a nonconceptual way, we begin to realize how our old ways have not served us very well.

EXCHANGING SELF AND OTHER

Once we learn to value the strength and practice of equanimity, we can then start to explore the next level of assessing where we are on the path. This next stage is learning to observe how much we are able to genuinely exchange ourselves and others, a practice that, first and foremost, must take place in our own mind.

The traditional practice of *tonglen*, of sending and taking, dives directly into the heart of this notion of exchange. In essence, we mentally take upon ourselves the suffering of others and send out our own positivity, virtue, good qualities and intentions, and our own tender heart. When we take in the suffering of others, we take it into our heart gladly and unreservedly in the visual form of a black cloud. As we breathe that black cloud into our heart, it immediately transforms into pure white light. We then send out all our positivity to others in the form of this white light emanating from our heart toward all beings. As we imagine the white light touching others, they immediately experience freedom, fulfillment, and complete ease. This taking and sending naturally rides upon our breath, in and out, in and out.

This time-tested method of tonglen works to reverse our deeply entrenched pattern of clinging to the self above all else. Some people can become nervous when they first hear about tonglen practice, concerned that it might bring them more pain. Pain can only occur as a result of negative deeds or negative intentions. Tonglen is a wholly virtuous and positive practice with love and compassion at its core. Doing tonglen accumulates tremendous merit, or positive energy, which in turn helps us to progress along the path. Done properly, tonglen cannot be a cause of more pain or negativity. Of course, we will feel compassion, and sometimes we can even be moved to tears when thinking about or taking in the suffering of beings. But these tears are a sign of our heart opening and expanding, a sign of shedding the small self and embracing the universal self. The practice of exchanging self and other cleanses us, leaving us much more available to others.

We must keep in mind that this practice is not something that we immediately try to execute in real life or off our meditation cushion, especially as a beginner. We practice this in our own mind and on our cushion as a means to truly exchange the exaggerated affection we have for the self for a more wholesome and universal affection toward all sentient beings. Incidentally, we don't exclude ourselves from this universal affection. It is just that we don't hold ourselves exclusively at the center of it all with everything catering only to us.

We can, of course, experiment with this practice of exchange in small physical ways, like offering our seat to another person on the train or bus, surrendering a parking spot to the other person, serving our loved ones the first portion of a meal we are sharing, or offering a friend a nice cup of tea before pouring our own. There are countless small, yet powerful and meaningful ways that we can train ourselves in the exchange of self and others every single day. When we feel the squeeze or pinch of giving another person our coveted parking spot, for example, we know we have hit the target. We have struck the right nerve. These small acts may seem minor, but if done with altruism, they can have a big effect. Not only do they affect our psychology and view of the world, they also can change the patterns in our brain and greatly expand and cleanse our heart of the sticky residues of self-centeredness.

Generally speaking, our habit is to immediately reject any suffering we may encounter and to gather any and all happiness or pleasure for the self without much consideration for how this may affect others. If we take a step back and look objectively, we can see that this approach has only worked to reinforce the ego and our ego-clinging. Tonglen makes a radical move to do the opposite. Instead of turning away and rejecting any suffering or pain that we may encounter, we seek to take upon ourselves even more. We breathe it in.

We can even do this with our own suffering and pain. Instead of pushing away unpleasant or painful emotions and mental or physical states, we breathe in the pain of those experiences. We can do this on behalf of ourselves and all others who are going through such pain and suffering. Approaching life's unwanted and painful events in this way— using our own pain as a reference, opening up to the pain and suffering of all beings, breathing that in as a black cloud that immediately transforms into white light, and then sending that light out to others, along with all of our positivity, virtue, and merit—this makes our pain truly useful. Instead of running away, numbing out, or distracting ourselves when something painful, uncomfortable, or undesirable arises, tonglen *uses* that experience as a means to open up to what all beings are experiencing. In the process, our own immediate pain or confusion is transformed into a source of benefit for ourselves and others. This is how the practice of tonglen creates an internal shift that can radically change our old habit of self-absorption.

Tonglen reduces our blind, unchallenged attachment to the self. All negative deeds, which return to create more suffering, stem from this blind attachment. All our fears and anxieties spring directly from this attachment and clinging to the self. When we are released, even just a little, from this grip of the self, we immediately experience the freedom of that release. Tonglen is, ultimately, a practice of loving kindness and compassion that reverses the entrenched, systemic habit of self-absorption. As we practice sending and taking, the grip of the self is confronted, penetrated, and then slowly dissipates. Disrupting our single-pointed attachment to the self, and therefore everything that springs from that attachment, inevitably brings us to the realization of the nature of selflessness.

When we first hear about tonglen or begin this practice, it may feel unnatural or counterintuitive. From the conventional, ego-based point of view, the exchange of self and other is completely revolutionary. But not only that, tonglen is the essence of profound wisdom and skillful means. What seems natural and intuitive to us now—clinging to the self first and foremost—has only served as the basis and source of all our suffering. We need nothing short of this revolutionary approach if we are to penetrate what we never considered penetrating before: our unquestioned clinging to the self. We also must know that however much we "sacrifice," or penetrate our attachment to the self, particularly internally, we personally experience that much freedom and ease.

As we let go of the self, or rather expand our self-attachment to include all sentient beings, particularly through the inner practice of tonglen, we find freedom and liberation right there. It has been said time and time again, "Exchanging self and other is only a practice for those who aspire to genuine freedom and liberation." If this is what we wish for, along with the ability to benefit others, tonglen is the one practice that we cannot do without. It is up to us and entirely in our hands. No one but ourselves can experience our own freedom or our own imprisonment.

It is helpful to remind ourselves that this is a gentle and gradual process. Nothing is forced or terribly difficult. We just need interest in what might lie beyond, or beneath, the conventional "me first" attitude. We need to be interested in bodhichitta and in living a larger, richer life. Our interest, curiosity, and willingness to try are key factors here.

CONSIDERING OTHERS AS MORE IMPORTANT THAN ONESELF

The last of the three ways of assessing our progress on the path is learning to consider others as more important than ourself. Let us examine why this makes sense. As we become more acquainted with the practices and the progression of considering ourselves and others as equal and then exchanging self and other, we begin to experience more freedom and ease. We feel the habitual grip of the self loosening and realize that grip is not as essential as we once believed. We can live quite well—much better, in fact—without everything being dictated by the shenpa of our small, self-centered self.

As we pursue and deepen our study of the teachings on emptiness and selflessness, we learn that there is no basis for our ego-clinging in the first place. Our clinging to a self or ego is merely based on a misperception: *tsul min yijé* in Tibetan. What this means is that we take our experiences of our body or form, our feelings, our conceptions, our mental formations, and our consciousnesses—known as our five *skandhas*—and arbitrarily lump them together, assigning to them an identity or self that we believe to be singular, permanent, and existing from its own side.

If we take this arbitrarily assigned identity and carefully examine it, however, we find that it has no real existence—meaning it does not exist in the way we cling to as a singular, permanent, and independent entity. The five skandhas have some relative functional existence in that we undeniably have a compounded physical body, we feel and think things, and so on. The notion of a "self," however, which we hold as "real"—meaning singular, permanent, and existing from its own side—has no findable existence outside of our habitual misperception, belief, and clinging to the presumed identity of a self that we lay on top of the collective five skandhas.

This contemplation is not something we simply "get" right away. We must first hear this—often repeatedly—and then we must carefully contemplate it over and over again. In fact, we never cease contemplating this topic. The more we study and examine, the more our understanding deepens and unfolds. First, we must accurately grasp the general idea and clarify any misunderstandings, and then we examine this for ourselves: *Can I find a self? Can I locate a singular, permanent entity that exists from its own side, inside or outside of the five skandhas?*

We never cling to a self outside of the five skandhas. For example, we don't hold a self to exist in our coffee table. So it is the five skandhas—our body, our feelings, our conceptions, our mental formations, and our consciousnesses—that we must thoroughly examine, one by one, in order to see firsthand if a self can be found as a singular, permanent, or independent entity.

We tend to cling to the self as either one with skandhas or as the owner of the skandhas. For instance, when we say, "I am going to the store," the *I* (or self) is held as one with the body that is going to the store. When we say, "My back hurts," we are implying that the self is the owner of the body, in this case our back. These assumptions are built into our language. Functionally, or for the sake of communication, these distinctions do not present a problem, but the unexamined assumption that a self truly exists is, ultimately speaking, the cause of all our suffering. Taking time to question this through personal examination is thus deeply liberating.

As I mentioned, we first look at our body, then our feelings, then our concepts or beliefs, then our thoughts, and finally our various consciousnesses—the five sensory consciousnesses of sight, smell, sound, taste, and touch; the sixth consciousness, which contains all mental events; the seventh consciousness, which holds the sense of "I" in all that we experience; and lastly our eighth consciousness, or the alaya. In all five skandhas, we want to examine this question: *Can*

I find a self residing there, particularly in the manner in which I cling to it—as singular, permanent, and existing from its own side?

Let's look at the body, or our physical form, as an example with which to begin this process of examination. Generally, we cling to our body as singular—we only buy one ticket for ourselves when we go to the movies. The body, nonetheless, has many parts—countless parts, in fact, and those parts can be broken down further and further into smaller parts. The body and all its parts are also constantly changing, in both gross and subtle ways. Most of us have heard that seven years from now all the cells in our body today will have been replaced after dying and being sloughed off by one or another of the body's processes of elimination. Whether or not this is completely accurate, we can still observe how much our bodies change, both inside and out, even in a single year. Where is the singular or permanent sense of self to be found in all of that?

Furthermore, this body did not just pop into existence all by itself. It was gifted to us by our mother's egg and our father's sperm. From the moment of our conception, it has been sustained by the continuous provision of fluids and nourishment, first in our mother's womb and then through a lifetime of consumption. We are kept warm, clothed, and sheltered through the efforts and lives of countless others. Where, in this complex web of dependency, is the independent, self-existing aspect of the self that we hold so dear? Thinking in this way initiates our examination to see whether we can find a singular, permanent, or self-existing aspect of the self residing anywhere in the skandha of our body or form, either in its parts or as a whole.

We similarly look for singular, permanent, and self-existing aspects of the self in our feelings, then our concepts or beliefs, then our thoughts, and finally in our various levels of consciousness. We may think, *I am not aware of clinging to the skandhas or myself as singular, permanent, and self-existing. Is all this examination really necessary?* It is helpful to understand that we do not consciously cling to a self in these three ways. It all happens automatically, emotionally, or subconsciously. These three ways of clinging, however, are precisely what make us *feel* that the self is real. Based on that feeling of assumed realness, we react to push away anything that threatens our sense of self and grasp after anything that we feel might cherish or support our sense of self.

These two tendencies of protecting and cherishing the self and the ensuing reactiveness that arises in our interactions with others are evidence of our unconscious misapprehension of, or belief in, a self. We may think, *I understand how there is no singular, permanent, or independent aspect of the self to be found in the skandhas. That makes sense. So now what?* It is great if we have a conceptual grasp of this profound teaching of the Buddha. But the true test of our understanding and realization comes in our ordinary day-to-day lives. What is happening in the world of our five kleshas and in our relationships with others? How do our aggression, desire, pride, jealousy, and deep mental fog manifest, particularly in relation to those closest to us?

Once our self-centered emotions arise, we usually act out before we can stop ourselves, and thus create negative karma, which returns to us as suffering. This is the mirror that shows us the depth of our understanding and realization. This is how we identify the work we still have to do. We therefore want to stay open and humble and continually search for any aspect of a singular, permanent, or independent self residing in the five skandhas. Alternating between using our critical intelligence, which researches our assumed belief in a self, and honest reflection on our personal experiences is how we progress on this path to freedom.

Not finding a self in the way in which we cling to it clears up our almost primordial misconception, or tsul min yijé—the erroneous assumption that a self, a real identity, resides in our skandhas. This is like pulling back the curtain on our ignorance to see what is really there. This "not finding" of a self in any of the three aspects of realness—that is, as singular, permanent, or existing from its own side—is the greatest discovery one can have on the Buddhist path. It is the beginning of the realization of *shunyata*, or emptiness—*tongpa nyi* in Tibetan.

Emptiness here is not a void or a nothingness—the images of void or nothingness are mere thoughts and mental pictures themselves. Emptiness has a very specific meaning: empty of how we cling to or hold things to be—empty of how we cling to our mind and body, our thoughts and mental states, including our emotions, and all physical form, as "real."

Discovering how all dependently originated phenomena are empty by nature is not like chipping away at the side of a mountain with a pick in order to see what lies at the center. It is self-study of our own mind and its essence or nature and of the nature of our skandhas. In other words, the careful examination of our mind and body—our physical form and the four mental skandhas.

The Buddha was probably not the first person to question our unconscious belief in the realness of all we encounter, but he pursued his examination of how we cling to a self and phenomena to its end. Through his meditation and examination, he realized the nature of his mind and all phenomena.

In discovering shunyata or the true nature of all appearances, the Buddha saw that all phenomena, internal and external, are empty of the three characteristics of realness. He saw that all phenomena appear and function interdependently and yet are empty by nature. This is the meaning of *illusory*: things appear and function perfectly and in accordance with the relative laws of cause and effect, yet they do not truly exist in the manner in which they appear. More specifically, they do not truly exist in the way in which we habitually perceive them and hold them to exist.

In Tibetan, *nangtsul* means "the way things appear," while *nétsul* refers to "the way things are." Generally, we relate only to the way things appear—meaning how we grasp and assume them to be—mainly because we have not received the hearing wisdom or the teachings on how to understand, discover, and relate to the way things are.

Once we come to understand, even conceptually, that all phenomena, including the self, are empty of any inherent existence—meaning that all appearances and what we hold to be real are merely designated by our own mind and its imputations—we simultaneously discover a great, immeasurable reserve of compassion for beings. As we progress, our understanding and realization unleash a boundless freedom within, and we discover tremendous space in our mind—and, therefore, in our interactions and relations with others. By "others" we do not mean human beings alone but all sentient beings—any creature with a mind that feels pain or joy, even on the most simplistic level.

While we may have an understanding and a growing realization of this, most others do not. There is thus a great need to care for others, to help them by any means necessary, and to consider them as more important than oneself—because, ultimately, we can. By virtue of our knowledge and understanding of selflessness and emptiness and our commitment to the practice of the four immeasurables, we are much more available to others. Our bodhichitta and the awakened state of mind that understands, even to a small degree, that all things are designated and empty by nature open up tremendous space in our heart to care for others. It is from this place that we work on the third level in our progress on the bodhisattva path: considering others to be more important than oneself.

This concludes the section of the text that cultivates awareness of the laziness of distracting preoccupations and unwholesome actions.

12

THE POWER OF PRAYER
AND ASPIRATION

We now move into the section of the text that is about cultivating awareness of the laziness of self-deprecation. This topic is covered in verses 17–30, which we will begin here and continue to discuss over the next several chapters.

17
"Oh, but how could I become enlightened?"
Don't excuse yourself with such despondency!
The Buddha, who declares the truth,
Has truly spoken and proclaimed

18
That if they bring forth strength of perseverance,
Even bees and flies
And gnats and grubs will gain
Supreme enlightenment so hard to find.

In the following fourteen verses, Shantideva focuses on cultivating a keen awareness of the laziness of self-deprecation, which manifests as low self-esteem. Remember, to find the way out of our confusion, we must first go into it and understand it. Shantideva begins this section of the chapter by dramatizing our self-deprecating thoughts: *I am not a good practitioner. I don't think I can be diligent like other people. It is so hard to spend time doing meditation.* Or we may think, *I don't want to change. I am fine the way I am.* Or, *I don't think I can do this, so I might as well not even try.* These sentiments can arise; and, of course, there is no problem with thoughts and feelings arising, whatever they may be. It is what we do next that calls for skill.

First, without suppressing any such thoughts or feelings, we must remember that we do not have to believe everything we think. We can instead remind ourselves that the *Tathagata*—the World-Awakened One—having no reason to lie, said that even flies, bees, and other bugs, if they give rise to the genuine intention to become liberated and benefit beings, will eventually become enlightened. The Buddha also said in the sutras, "All things are circumstantial. All circumstances evolve according to our intention. With intention, diligent effort, and prayer or aspiration, we can make our way to where we wish to go.

In our modern culture many people have some confusion about, and even aversion to, prayer. I don't doubt that there are valid reasons for this. Nonetheless, let's look more closely at what prayer means in Buddhism. In the context of the Dharma, prayer is the purest form of aspiration coming directly from our heart. We have many prayers that we recite each day and some that we say from time to time. We recite them to train the direction of our aspirations and to give them a clear, virtuous pathway forward.

Our prayers and aspirations have the potential to affect us in many powerful ways. It is thus helpful to know the prayers of great compassionate beings like the Buddha or Shantideva. Their prayers give us insight into what they most valued and what was possible from their point of view. Reciting their prayers reveals the direction toward which they aimed and gives us a script to follow so that we can adopt the same mindset and follow in their footsteps. Without such prayers and aspirations, we wouldn't know what to aspire to or pray for outside of the limited world of our likes, dislikes, and preferences. We wouldn't know what we are capable of or that we could even make such aspirations, much less what their results could possibly be. As we recite such prayers and aspirations, we gradually begin to make them our own. As we deepen our knowledge of and our connection to what we are reciting, the strength of that ownership naturally increases.

When we feel unhappy, discontented, or on edge, these prayers and aspirations provide us with an alternative—especially the prayers and aspirations of the four immeasurables. When edginess, irritation, or discontentment arise, if we notice our mindset and our internal dialogue, we will usually find we are quite self-absorbed in our circular storylines. This self-absorption can be subjectively hard to notice, but it is the very thing that feeds our discontentment and feelings of stuckness.

Reciting the prayer "May all beings attain happiness and the causes and conditions of happiness" conceptually reminds us that all beings are similarly striving to be happy and free of suffering. We are reminded that we are all equal in our state of sentience, and this opens our heart a bit. Reciting this prayer several times forces us to slow down and to more genuinely consider loving kindness toward all beings. It interrupts the habitual momentum of our broken-record thought patterns of self-loathing, self-disparagement, and fixation.

It is not that we ignore or suppress our own suffering. The four immeasurables prayer impels us instead to use our own experience of suffering as a vehicle to genuinely open up to others. Furthermore, acknowledging others' suffering and their need for happiness enables us to pray that their pain be burned up and exhausted by our own experience of pain or suffering. This dramatically changes how we experience our own suffering, and we come to see that we can use any painful or undesired experience as an opportunity to deepen the four immeasurables and tonglen practice. The side effect of this practice is that it naturally remedies our own habit of self-centeredness—the cause of all our pain.

Cultivating loving kindness engenders an energy that lifts us up, elevates our state of mind, and warms our heart. Cultivating compassion or deep empathy for the suffering of beings and praying that all their suffering and its causes be exhausted through our own experience of pain expands our heart, getting us in touch with the state of all beings in samsara. We are on the path and have made the bodhisattva's commitment to attain enlightenment for the benefit of all other sentient beings.

Aspirations and prayers like the four immeasurables and tonglen are powerful tools that can awaken and transform our mind. That is why the *Seven Points of Mind Training* says, "Start with the *words* of lojong." We begin with the prayers of great beings to establish a structure and means to transform our mind, rather than thinking that we first need to transform our mind in order to make prayers. Going about it in this order is an important distinction on the bodhisattva's path.

Aspirations connect us not only to beings who are suffering but also to those who are doing good things in the world and are already helping others. We can take a moment and consider all the people around the world who get up early every day to go to work or go about their daily activities in the service of others. Of course, their work supports their livelihood, but that is not what they hold in their mind each day as they get ready to leave home. They are thinking of the day ahead, what they are working on, what they hope to accomplish or do. Think of all the nurses and schoolteachers, street cleaners and trash collectors, doctors and technicians working in war-torn countries or in local clinics and hospitals, social workers helping families and individuals, aid volunteers, mothers and fathers and caregivers, checkout clerks at the market, people who drive buses, taxis, *tuk-tuks*, trains, and Ubers, technicians who keep our cities supplied with electricity, water, and gas, and everyone else who does things to help others in ordinary and extraordinary ways. We can make sincere and heartfelt prayers that they continue to do their jobs well and help others, especially in places where there is great suffering. Rather than taking all of this for granted, we can support these individuals in our prayers and aspirations, wishing them to live long and to continue to do their work with altruism, free of hindrances. Making prayers and aspirations is a powerful use of our mind and its capacity. This is a potent energy to put out into the world.

As mentioned earlier, there is no magic in diligence. It is not as though from one day to the next we can let go of all our distracting preoccupations and laziness and miraculously transform ourselves into having joyful exertion in all we do. Diligence happens through using our mind—through honest self-reflection and self-determination, which comes from inspiring ourselves. Self-inspiration is only genuine if we know what we can gain and what we have to lose. Contemplating what we have to gain motivates us, and contemplating what we have to lose also spurs us on.

Möpa means aspiration, which includes our motivation or intention. It is a simple word, but its meaning contains the depth of intelligent self-reflection. Contemplating the pros and cons, or gains and losses, clarifies our mind and inspires us. Our self-inspiration, or möpa, allows us to apply ourselves with greater depth and motivation, with joy at the heart of whatever we do. In the case of the third type of laziness—that of self-denigration—the remedy is self-confidence.

13

SELF-CONFIDENCE COMES FROM TWO SOURCES

As with any endeavor, we must first learn the ropes and how things are done. This is the first source of self-confidence. It applies to conventional skills, as well as to learning the Dharma. In the Dharma, we have a sense that there is a vast body of wisdom and skillful means that allows us to achieve what we wish on the path. This wisdom and skillful means are available to anyone who has genuine interest, but we must learn how to properly relate to them—how to identify, engage, and apply them. We therefore look to those who have gone before us, examining and studying how they did it.

If we want to get good at a sport, we can study how those who excel in that sport have trained, and we can learn to train like them. First we have to learn the rules. Then we study players we admire or who have been successful in that sport. What wisdom and skillful means did they use, how did they employ the rules of the game, and what examples did they set for others to follow? By examining, learning, and absorbing, we adopt the knowledge and skill of those we most admire.

Wisdom is understanding how it is all done, grasping the scope and the general process, and getting an overall picture of how successful people have accomplished their goals. Skillful means is learning how to bring that general scope, understanding, and process into our lives, integrating all of that as an active participant. This is how we come to gain confidence. Genuine confidence is based on bringing wisdom and skillful means together, and then slowly expanding upon them. This process has nothing to do with ego, but as with anything, ego can always sneak in and hijack it all. So we want to be mindful of this.

In the case of the Dharma, we must have some trust in order to enter the path. Trust in what? In the wisdom and skillful means that have been successfully passed down from teachers to disciples for generations. As we gain experience over time, we come to adopt such wisdom and skillful means as our own. As stated in the teachings, "Everything is imitation. Whoever imitates the best, becomes the best." This refers to cultivating the wisdom and skillful means of the Dharma. We are not born endowed with all knowledge and abilities. Life is a continual process of gaining wisdom and adopting skillful means in all fields and then exploring how to integrate what we learn.

Growing up, we imitate everyone around us to become integrated into our society and culture. Imitating others is not a new idea. It is something we already do in every aspect of our lives. So rather than dwelling on insecurity or self-denigration, we can consciously turn our mind toward imitating the bodhisattvas and adopting their approach. There is no better set of values or ideals to imitate than those of the buddhas and bodhisattvas, particularly their teachings on the four immeasurables.

The second source of self-confidence is knowing—and reminding ourselves—that nothing is static. With time and practice, everything gets easier. Here we want to think to ourselves, *Those who have gone before me have accomplished what they did through wisdom and skillful means as a source of strength and clarity, particularly when facing whatever task lay ahead of them. It didn't just come to them, nor were they born knowing how to do it all. It is through practice that they succeeded and became good at what they did—and I can do this too.*

Look back on your own life. You have surely done many things that you learned by relying on various kinds of wisdom and skillful means. Now many of those things, like driving for instance, have become second nature to you. You weren't born knowing how to do all those things, but you learned.

There is no logical reason to dwell on our insecurities unless we want to stay there as a form of laziness or self-attachment or because it is simply more familiar to succumb to that thought pattern than to change. It is not that such thoughts or feelings shouldn't or won't come up for us; we just don't have to give in to them or believe them to be our absolute truth. When you began learning how to drive, did you feel some fear and trepidation? Most likely. Did you also feel confident that you would be able to learn, especially knowing that countless others had successfully done so before you? Perhaps you thought to yourself, *Everybody learns how to drive, so why not me?* Now we don't think about it at all. We just get in our car and go. Maybe we don't remember thinking these things consciously, but that thought process was most likely in our mind at some time.

The point is that we need some level of self-confidence in just about every area of our life. Self-confidence is an emotional experience and state of mind. All emotions and experiences arise from their own causes and conditions. The causes and conditions of confidence on the path are, first, developing trust in the wisdom and skillful means of the Dharma and, second, knowing that as we apply ourselves to something and gain personal experience it naturally becomes easier and easier. These are the two sources of self-confidence for everyone, at every level of the path. When we become insecure or start down the path of self-denigration, we must actively call to mind and employ these two pillars of self-confidence.

14

DHARMA PRACTICE

Neurosis and Remedy

The practice of Dharma comes down to neurosis versus remedy. First we must recognize the neurosis, and then we need to learn how to appropriately apply the remedy. Only one thought at a time can occur in our mind stream. As we become aware of the neurosis and apply the remedy, the remedy becomes integrated into our mind stream. The more we apply the remedy, the more precedence it takes. This is how any neurosis is overcome.

If we recall the four factors that allow us to create or overcome habits, the same four apply to overcoming neurosis: (1) doing something repeatedly and (2) in a more intensive manner, in this case consistently and sincerely applying a remedy when our neurosis arises; (3) the lack of a counteragent, in this case refraining from indulging the neurosis; and (4) the availability of the field, which here is vigilantly applying ourselves whenever our neurosis arises.

In all of this, we must be sure that we do in fact want to overcome our neurosis and confusion. Success depends first and foremost on our interest and in wanting to change for the better. This is a conscious choice, meaning we are conscious of the pros of changing for the better and the cons of staying in the same rut. We need that interest, along with the consciousness of how our neurosis does not serve us.

Relating to any neurosis and applying appropriate remedies all happen within the context of what we want to accomplish in our life. We work on understanding what supports that process. Knowing that all beings, including ourselves, inherently possess Buddha nature is very supportive to our aspiration to find genuine freedom and ease. Besides this basic potential of Buddha nature that we all possess, the active cause of liberation is generating bodhichitta. And the active cause for generating bodhichitta is cultivating altruism.

We all have altruism. It is part of our makeup. Even evil people have altruism—perhaps not toward what they would destroy but toward themselves or those who are on their side. We can see inherent altruism in many animals as well. Even vicious, poisonous snakes have altruism and love for their young. Consciously practicing and cultivating altruism sows a precious seed. It is precious because it ripens our deepest potential: to attain enlightenment for the benefit of all sentient beings.

Recently I saw a short video in which a family of pigs was trying to push a writhing fish back into the water. The fish had somehow jumped out of the water and was on dry land. The pigs knew that the water was the fish's home and that it needed to return there to survive. This shows the innate altruism that all beings possess. Even if beings do horrible, harmful things, they still have this quality somewhere inside. It is a matter of recognizing it and learning to give it weight and significance.

Much of the Dharma unfolds based on self-study. What are we studying? We study the teachings on the nature and the functions of the mind, and then we study our neuroses, our habits, our ignorance, and our suffering. Neuroses become powerful because of the emotions that accompany our various neurotic states of mind. Destructive emotions, or the kleshas, are always based on the belief in a self, which we hold as intrinsically real and separate from everything else. That separateness is held in place by the threefold assumption in the realness of self—namely that the self is singular, permanent, and exists from its own side. This belief operates unconsciously in our mind stream. As we study the Dharma, we learn about this and then we come to see how it is true in our own experience. The Dharma doesn't stop there, though. Along with showing us our neurosis and how habitual patterns are formed, the

Dharma also acquaints us with our strength, the power of our mind's motivation, and especially our innate potential. This all unfolds based on the three wisdoms: hearing wisdom, contemplative wisdom, and meditative wisdom.

In terms of motivation, we have spoken of how impermanence and death motivate and self-inspire us. The Dharma further self-inspires us with the feeling that everything is doable. As verse 18 states in its quote from the Buddha, "Even bees and flies and gnats and grubs" can attain the state of enlightenment. We all possess an innate potential to wake up, to overcome our ignorance. So we study our mind in light of the teachings and the three wisdoms, learning to integrate the remedy into our mind stream and overcome the neurosis.

Society and technology have changed over the years and centuries, but how human emotions function, how our states of mind manifest, the mind's fundamental makeup and its potential—those have not changed. That is why this eighth-century text is still applicable to us in the twenty-first century: we are all basically the same. When we come to know ourselves through the three wisdoms of the Dharma, we naturally come to understand much of humanity and other sentient beings as well.

19
And if, by birth and lineage of humankind,
I'm able to distinguish good from ill,
And do not leave aside the Bodhisattva deeds,
Why should I not attain the state of Buddhahood?

If we doubt that we can be successful on the spiritual path because we think we don't have what it takes to attain liberation or to succeed, Shantideva is here to remind us that if we do not abandon the path of the bodhisattva, we, along with the smallest living creatures, can attain enlightenment and liberation—if we apply ourselves well.

The Tibetan term for a human being, *nashé döngo*, means "one who can hear and understand, reply and communicate." Animals can also do this to a certain degree. But the depth of their ability to understand

and communicate differs quite a bit from humans. Even though they have Buddha nature and a certain degree of natural altruism, it is not possible for an animal or an insect to understand the nature of the absolute truth or, on the relative level, the practice of equalizing self and others. Their inability also extends to worldly activities: they can't build machines or make a fire to cook food and stay warm.

The reason we humans have these abilities is that our *chörab namjé kyi shérab*, or our discriminative intelligence, is more developed due to our birth in a human body. Human beings are endowed with an innate ability to know what is favorable and what is not, what is supportive and what is not. We can assess this in the moment, and we can project ahead and discern this for the future. We may not always act accordingly—we definitely still have ignorance, habitual patterns, and neurosis, which significantly veil our intelligence—but we also know what helps and what harms us. That basic ability to know and project ahead is inherently there. It is important to acknowledge that we possess this innate level of critical intelligence and take heart.

20

"That I must give away my life and limbs
Alarms and frightens me"—if so you say,
Your terror is misplaced. Confused,
You fail to see what's hard and what is easy.

21

For myriads of ages, measureless, uncounted,
Your body has been cut, impaled,
Burned, torn—for times past numbering!
Yet none of this has brought you Buddhahood.

22

The hardships suffered on the path to Buddhahood
Are limited in their extent
And likened to the pain of an incision
Made to cure the harms of inward ills.

23

And all our doctors cure disease
By means of bitter remedies.
Likewise, to destroy a vast amount of pain,
We should be patient with our little hurts.

24

And yet the Supreme Healer does not use,
Like them, these common remedies.
With ways of extreme tenderness
He soothes away intense and boundless suffering.

We have been born as a human being, and we have the human intelligence that recognizes what is beneficial and what is harmful. So we want to ask ourselves, *Why can't I also apply that knowledge to my path and attain liberation?* If we think that it is too hard to do what bodhisattvas do on the path, giving their limbs and such to beings in need, Shantideva challenges our assumptions, saying that we have not carefully thought this through. In samsara, over the course of our countless lives and even to a degree in this present life, we have been beaten and cut, burned alive and pounded. Born as fish and animals, we have been eaten and torn to bits innumerable times. The Buddha said, "If all the limbs that we have lost were to be piled up together, that pile would be bigger than Mt. Meru; if all the tears we have shed were to be collected it would make a body of water larger than all the oceans combined." Yet we have nothing to show for having gone through all this suffering, misery, pain, and loss. In the case of the *bodhisattvayana*, or the path of the bodhisattva, yes, it is true that the bodhisattva must give limbs and many other things, but this kind of generosity happens much later on the path, and only when one is realized and thus immune to the kind of suffering we might imagine such feats of generosity to inflict.

In light of these teachings on the advanced practices of the bodhisattva's path, I find an interesting irony to consider regarding how we culturally perceive extreme physical hardships, such as having our limbs amputated or our organs removed. Many of us willingly, indeed gratefully, subject ourselves to surgeries, operations, and various types of invasive procedures. Sometimes these procedures are not performed for lifesaving measures but merely to look a few years younger or to change the shape of our body. Doctors we barely know walk in with their masks and white jackets and examine us under bright lights; nurses in their own scrubs and gloves rush in and out as if they were in a train station; and all the while, we lie there anxiously wondering, *Will I be alive at the end of all this?* The anesthesiologist, again someone we hardly know and will likely never see again, comes in with a chart and a serious demeanor, takes various measurements, asks us a few short questions, and puts us to sleep. Surgeons proceed to cut us open with sharp instruments and even saws, suction out our blood and other fluids, remove organs, put metal plates in our joints or stents in our veins and ducts, and then sew us back up like a sack. Our body and our very life are completely in these people's hands. One small slip or miscalculation can put an end to our life right there. It is all very intimidating. The smell of hospitals alone is intimidating. But we, more or less, willingly go and submit ourselves to all of this. We are glad to have a cancerous organ taken out, or to donate a kidney if a loved one is in need, or get a facelift if we think we are looking too old and saggy.

THE BUDDHA'S TEACHINGS ARE GENTLE

Following the bodhisattva path and the Buddha's advice is not like this. The Buddha's teachings are gentle, and the Dharma is gentle; they are not at all like undergoing surgeries or medical procedures—lifesaving as they may be. This reflection is meant to show us how we can bear something difficult if the benefit is clear and we understand what is happening. Here, the bodhisattva practice is not just enduring pain as a martyr or to get attention from the world. Nor is it the ordinary removal of a cancerous tumor or plastic surgery. It is ultimately a practice of transcending samsara altogether. It is about letting go of the self, letting go of the greatest "tumor" or affliction of them all, the very thing that causes all our own and others' suffering: clinging to the self.

The tender methods of the Buddha to which Shantideva refers specifically are the practices of aspiration bodhichitta and application bodhichitta. This means the practice of the four immeasurables, which gives birth to aspiration bodhichitta—the wish to attain enlightenment for the benefit of all sentient beings—and then applying our aspiration bodhichitta through the practice of the six paramitas. The progression of the four immeasurables and our bodhichitta practices can be measured by internal observation and assessment. Aspiration bodhichitta is not something that we try to show off outwardly. Instead, we work internally to develop our heart and the value system of bodhichitta, which is different from that of the conventional consensus.

Developing our heart and our strength based on the values of the bodhisattva path generates tremendous self-confidence. With this self-confidence, we mount and ride the horse of our aspiration and application bodhichitta practices and travel from bliss to bliss. Our self-confidence gives us further strength to overcome our laziness, distraction, low self-esteem, and lethargy. This combination of self-confidence and strength continually awakens our mind and softens our heart.

Sometimes we may long to "do" things, to get active in the world or to test ourselves. This is a wonderful aspiration, and ultimately we want to encourage this vision. It is equally important, however, to trust that opportunities to benefit others will naturally arise as we develop our own inner clarity and strength. As these occasions arise, we will be ready—we won't be easily overwhelmed or burned out by the sometimes strenuous demands of benefiting beings. That inner reservoir of strength and clarity comes not from our willpower or ego drive. It comes from the inner practice of the four immeasurables and the growing strength of our aspiration and application bodhichitta practices.

Once again, we are not asked, nor is it required, to engage in various forms of extraordinary generosity until it comes naturally. Bodhisattvas would not do what they do if it were truly painful. It is said that if pain truly existed, the bodhisattva would not be able to bear a single great deed among the many that they undertake for the sake of beings. So we must respect the process of the bodhisattva path. We must humbly work on developing our self-confidence and strength, learning first on our cushion the practice of exchange and tonglen. One day we will be there to give someone what they need, even parts of our own body, without feeling threatened or that we are losing anything of value. Meanwhile, the inner training of our heart and mind is essential and also contributes tremendous positivity to the world. The Buddha's teachings are thus soothing, effective, and truthful. The medicine of the Buddhadharma effectively remedies our neuroses and cures our most serious illness: our ignorance and self-importance.

25
Our guide instructs us to begin
By giving vegetable greens or other little things,
That later, step by step, the habit once acquired,
We may be able to donate our very flesh.

26
For when we truly feel
Our bodies are no different from the given herbs,
What hardship can there be
In giving up, relinquishing, our very flesh?

If someone is stingy and does not want to be generous or give anything away, the Buddha doesn't say, "You must give everything, now!" There is a story of a wealthy but stingy businessman who could not bear to give anything to anyone. Instead of scolding him, the Buddha suggested that he first give from one hand to the other, imagining himself as the giving hand and the hand that received as someone else. The man struggled even to give from his one hand to the other. He couldn't bear to let go, thinking he was losing something by giving it away. Luckily, he was honest, humble, and open to the Buddha's instructions, so he kept trying. Eventually the gesture and imprint of giving began to take root, and he was able to give from his right hand to his left. To his surprise, he felt good after doing this—lighter and freer. He then ventured to give small gifts to his loved ones. Again, to his surprise, he liked it. As time went on, he gave to the poor and to those in need, and he eventually became one of the greatest patrons of the Buddhadharma itself, supporting many monks and nuns on the path.

Once a bodhisattva enters the first *bhumi*, or stage of the bodhisattva's path, due to the power of their realization of emptiness and selflessness, which is still not complete until the tenth bhumi, they no longer suffer in the same way as ordinary beings. Conventional beings like us wander in samsara and are endlessly subject to suffering, repeatedly and pointlessly losing our limbs and life. The practice of taking on hardships for the sake of progressing on the path of liberation is meaningful—like taking the doctor's medicine when we are ill. We willingly take the treatment, knowing that this is how we recover our health. If we see the reason for being generous and its benefit—not only for the beneficiary but also as a great meritorious means to progress on the bodhisattva path and realize the perfection of generosity—then generosity becomes easier and easier. At some point, we can even come to see this dear body of ours as illusory and gladly give it away, just like offering a meal to a hungry person.

For bodhisattvas on the bhumis, it is like this. They can give away their limbs as they might give away some herbs or a piece of fruit. Once again, this is not an immediate result of generosity practice but a gradual one that is integrated with the practice and realization of emptiness. The gradual process of the path allows our mind to digest the teachings, thus incorporating and understanding the point of everything we do. To become free from the suffering of samsara altogether, we learn to welcome small hardships and the gradual practices of the bodhisattva's way of life as a means to reap great freedom and benefit in the end.

By comparison, if we have an illness like colon or breast cancer, we first have to go to the hospital and have the tumor removed. Having the cancerous tissue removed is the fast part; then we have to recover. That is a long and often difficult process, usually taking many months until we feel normal again. Those of you who have faced such circumstances or cared for others who have know this firsthand. The practice of Dharma is comparatively easy, not at all harsh like many of the medical treatments we welcome into our lives. In the practice of Dharma and the bodhisattva path, to heal ourselves from the sickness of samsara we simply sit on a comfortable cushion and work with our mind and what arises. Just as we welcome conventional medical methods to cure the body's ills, we can also welcome what is soft and gentle, the medicine of the Buddha's bodhichitta teachings, as a means to cure ourselves from the vicious illness of samsara.

The Buddha's teachings are gradual. Being generous is not compulsory, but it is to our own benefit to practice the perfection of generosity in stages. As we are ready to go a little further, and then further yet, we come to realize that our own open and generous heart, which is there to meet the needs of beings and is not threatened by anything, is the greatest wealth we could possibly possess. This itself is the perfection of generosity, the first of the paramitas.

15

HOW THE BODHISATTVA ELIMINATES PHYSICAL AND MENTAL SUFFERING

27
Sin has been abandoned, thus there is no pain;
Through having wisdom there is no more sorrow.
For so it is that mind and body both
Are injured by false views and sinfulness.

From the Buddhist point of view, suffering, whether physical or mental, is a by-product of past harmful actions. In other words, suffering is a by-product of negative karma, meaning that, in the past, we have engaged in deeds that caused harm or inflicted pain on other living beings. That said, what is done is done. So now the question is: How, with this present knowledge, can we move forward? Honest acknowledgment and remorse over past wrongdoing and the self-reflective question of how to proceed in accord with the Dharma can change how things unfold.

Going forward, the bodhisattva may have to experience the effect of past actions as a means of burning or exhausting the seeds of past negative deeds. Renouncing and refraining from harming others from this point on prevent generating any further causes of suffering. Generally speaking, mental suffering comes from having indulged in emotions such as aggression, jealousy, pride, greed, scorn, and so forth, while physical suffering arises as an effect of having harmed others in the past. Our disturbing emotions, or kleshas, are rooted in our unchecked self-cherishing and self-protection and churned up by our unbridled chains of thought. As we learn to meditate on the four immeasurables and contemplate the emptiness of self and phenomena, the ground of mental suffering becomes less and less solid.

As we personally familiarize ourselves with the reasoning of self-lessness and emptiness, our thoughts, which we have always held as "real," become less solid. We experience them as illusory. *Illusory* here means that things do not exist as they appear. The world of the self—our self-protection and self-cherishing—is not as solid as we assume and hold it to be. Our thoughts that are like fire and our emotions that are like smoke arising from that fire are also not as real and solid as we hold them to be. Knowing this conceptually is a helpful reference point, but to discover this for ourselves, we must progress from our hearing wisdom into the more personal process of contemplative and meditative wisdom. In other words, we must develop firsthand insight into the nature of our thoughts and emotions, beyond conceptually labeling things as illusory or not existing as they appear. This process of discovery gives us tremendous room and choice to work with our habitual patterns and our arising thoughts and emotions without re-jecting anything.

The result and benefit of practicing emptiness and compassion are that, when karmic seeds ripen, we have the strength and perspective to engage whatever arises with joy as a means to purify and exhaust those seeds. For the bodhisattva, it is not just about one's own karmic seeds or the fruit of those seeds alone. The bodhisattva aspires to purify the neg-ative karma of all beings who are suffering or experiencing the ripening of past negative deeds. This courageous aspiration is important, as it is a way to exercise the authenticity of our understanding. In our mind, we aspire to take on the suffering and pain of all beings, thereby purifying their negative karma without a single exception. This is the courage of a bodhisattva. Adopting the bodhisattva's brave heart as our own protects us from mindlessly engaging in self-centered states of mind and klesha activity, and thus prevents us from sowing further seeds of mental suffering and sorrow.

As all things are dependently originated, when we remove the cause of something, the effect is no longer there. Without a seed, there can be no fruit. Seeds of suffering, physical or mental, are sown when, due to our ignorance, we harm another being. That is the cause. As the bodhisattva progresses on the path of the three wisdoms, ignorance is slowly eradicated along with self-clinging tendencies. As we abandon the negativity of harming others, there is no cause to experience physical suffering. As we realize the egolessness of self and work with our kleshas, we slowly eradicate the cause of emotional suffering.

It is worth repeating: when there is no seed, there can be no fruit. We don't expect to be free of suffering all at once, but with time and diligent effort toward understanding and developing insight into the emptiness teachings and our consistent practice of compassion, particularly of the four immeasurables, we experience a change in our being. Knowing this, we want to do our best and strive to put all of this into practice.

28

Merit is the true cause of the body's ease,
While happiness of mind is had through understanding.
What can sadden those who have compassion,
Who remain within samsara for the sake of beings?

In addition to abandoning the negativity of harming others, physical and mental well-being comes from generating merit. Merit or *sönam* is the practice of virtue, of engaging in positive deeds for the benefit of others. Merit is generated based on knowing how to work with our mind and emotions in the deepest sense. In other words, we develop our understanding of how to integrate our mind with the practice of the four immeasurables and realize the emptiness of self and phenomena. Developing this level of integration is itself a source of joy.

Bodhisattvas, or aspiring bodhisattvas, may live in samsara for the benefit of others, but they are like lotus flowers. As we discussed, lotuses do not grow in dry ground. They flourish best in a muddy swamp, but the stain of the mud never touches or affects the purity of their petals. The lotus always floats above the murky water. Bodhisattvas similarly live joyfully while serving beings in samsara, thereby growing in their view and realization of emptiness and their practice of compassion. They do this best while living in the direst conditions of samsara. The bodhisattva, therefore, never rejects anything that arises but always seeks to find integration and realization with the sole aim of benefiting beings and further purifying their own ignorance. That is the deepest form of working with one's mind, and thus the greatest source of accumulating merit.

29

For through their power of bodhichitta,
Former sins are totally consumed,
And merit, ocean-vast, is gathered in,
It's therefore said that they excel the shrāvakas.

30

Mounted on the horse of bodhichitta,
Which puts to flight all mournful weariness,
What lucid person could be in despair
Proceeding in this way from joy to joy?

We may have heard how a bodhisattva comes back to samsara again and again, and we may think, *There is just so much suffering in samsara, why would anyone want to come back to this, especially if they had the choice? Who wouldn't want true and lasting peace if they had the chance to obtain that?* This could be seen, in part, as the view of the *shravakas*, the practitioners of the Basic Vehicle. The *shravakayana* as a path is extremely profound. It flourished greatly during the time of the Buddha and is the basis for the Buddhist path. The bodhisattva path, however, takes a wider perspective. Whereas the shravaka seeks to be free from the suffering of samsara by realizing the egolessness of the self, the bodhisattva expands this to include the egolessness of all phenomena, meaning the whole of our subjective and objective existence.

Furthermore, where the shravakas seek the peace of nirvana for themselves, the bodhisattva's motivation is to attain liberation for the benefit of all sentient beings. This motivation, coupled with the expanded view of the egolessness of self and phenomena, is the foundation for the emptiness teachings of the Mahayana path. It is said that the bodhisattva does not fall into either extreme—that of being lost in the suffering of samsara or of longing for the peace of nirvana for oneself alone. Instead, with courage, self-confidence, strength, and the perspective of the Middle Way, bodhisattvas joyfully dive back into the ocean of samsara, compassionately working for the benefit of all beings while perfecting their own accumulation of wisdom and merit. Like the stalk providing nutrients to the lotus growing out of the mud, the skillful means of the bodhisattvas' motivation and commitment keep them buoyant and unstained while living in the confusion and suffering of samsara.

Integrating the wisdom of this greater motivation and skillful means generates tremendous merit, thus eliminating both physical and mental suffering. Even coming back into samsara again and again, the bodhisattva who practices the Middle Way does not suffer. Look at the examples of great bodhisattvas, even in our own lifetime. His Holiness the Dalai Lama lost his country and his home and has faced so much hardship, including the ongoing destruction of his people's culture and heritage. He escaped Tibet with only his life in order to seek refuge in India and for all these years has served others while carrying the sorrow and loss of his people. But is he known for his despair and anger? No. He is known the world over for his joy and compassion and for his gentle playfulness with everyone he meets. There are few in this world who have faced, and continue to face, such circumstances. What keeps him afloat? He openly speaks of his reliance on the bodhichitta teachings, and in particular how much he depends on *The Way of the Bodhisattva* to see him through.

Another recent example is the Sixteenth Karmapa. As he was dying of stomach cancer in a hospital in Zion, Illinois, someone asked him how he was doing. He said, "No pain, no pain." And to another person who later asked the same question, he famously said, "Nothing happens." He remained cheerful and buoyant throughout the process of passing from this world.

Both of these people, and countless others, exhibit joy in the face of immeasurable suffering. How do they do that? Are they blessed souls or extraterrestrial beings endowed with special powers? I don't think so. They are flesh and blood human beings with a mind, just like you and me. One thing they have that is different, however, is an unwavering conviction in the basic goodness of all beings, along with a relentless pursuit of the bodhisattva path, as outlined in Shantideva's teachings in this book. Although they live in the midst of samsara and are committed to benefiting beings, their practice of compassion and emptiness means that nothing is tragic or devastating for them, nothing ultimately brings them down. It is all joyful and meaningful, all a process of growth and realization. They remain in samsara with great courage and joy to increase the breadth of their bodhichitta, work on their bodhisattva vow, further purify their obscurations, and exhaust all their negative karma with the sole motivation of serving others. Because this process is not focused on the self, the bodhisattva's self-confidence, strength, and wider perspective all continue to grow immeasurably. This is what makes the bodhisattvayana more expeditious, effective, and sophisticated than the shravakayana, profound and foundational though it is.

Bodhisattvas come into this world of suffering to bring benefit to beings and progress along their own path of wisdom and compassion, so that they may become more agile and effective in helping others. Their strength and courage are rooted in the realization of emptiness and their practice of compassion. The realization of emptiness immunizes them to physical and mental suffering, while their compassion compels them to live in the world and serve others.

Bodhisattvas are thus never despondent, nor are they averse to confronting suffering. They live amid the suffering of samsara with the absolute bodhichitta practice as their in-meditation training, and in the post-meditation they exercise their compassion at every opportunity. As Chandrakirti says in the *Introduction to the Middle Way*, "Like a swan with the two wings of wisdom and compassion, the bodhisattva glides from bliss to bliss." Of course, it takes diligence and discipline to engage in the bodhisattva path and overcome one's obstacles, but one's effort returns as great benefit to others and great joy for oneself, both in this life and in all future lives to come.

This concludes the section of the text that cultivates awareness of the laziness of self-deprecation. This also completes the verses of the Diligence Chapter that elucidate the three types of laziness. We now shift gears and move into the solution for how to remedy our laziness: the antidote of the four allies and two strengths.

16

THE ANTIDOTE TO LAZINESS

The Four Allies and the Two Strengths

Verses 31 and 32 introduce us to the four allies and the two strengths which outline the remedies to our laziness.

31
The forces that secure the good of beings
Are aspiration, steadfastness, relinquishment, and joy.
Aspiration grows through fear of suffering
And contemplation of the benefits to be attained.

32
Therefore leaving everything that is adverse to it,
I'll labor to increase my diligence,
Through aspiration and self-confidence, relinquishment
    and joy,
By strength of earnest application and exertion of control.

When bodhisattvas face challenges from the three kinds of laziness, or from anything else, they don't merely ride things out waiting for change. They actively employ tools and remedies, enlisting assistance to skillfully work with whatever is arising. Having explored and come to understand how laziness manifests through its three aspects, Shantideva now formally introduces the four allies. They are "allies" because they support us on the path and help us when the going gets tough. These four allies are how we apply the practice of diligence. In addition to the four allies, Shantideva teaches us about the two strengths, which further enhance our ability to overcome challenges and proceed in the direction we wish to go. Together, the four allies and the two strengths are the precise methods of how we go about relating to challenges, not only in our Dharma practice but in all areas of our lives.

The four allies are aspiration, steadfastness through developing self-confidence, joy, and resting or taking short breaks. In Tibetan, these four allies are möpa, *tenpa*, *gawa*, and *dorwa*.

Möpa, or aspiration, is the first ally. We have discussed self-inspiration or aspiration in relation to the laziness of distracting activities, so this topic will be familiar. Möpa arises from first learning how to discern and consider the pros and cons of anything that we are doing or wish to do. We imagine what it would be like to accomplish what we aspire to and what it would be like not to accomplish that thing. Playing this out in our mind brings a certain clarity and naturally leads to wholesome self-inspiration. This gets us going from inside once we have a clear picture in our mind about the pros and cons of a given endeavor. When we internally understand the pros and cons of a situation and its outcome, we don't necessarily need pep talks from our friends or inspiring sayings on our refrigerator to motivate us.

If we are clear about what we wish to achieve, we can then generate the aspiration to progress in that direction. It is like riding a bike. If we turn our head and consciously look in the direction we wish to go, our body and the bike naturally take us there. We first have to know where we want to go. Our inspiration or clarity can't come from the head alone, however. An inspired heart is also necessary. Aspiration and self-inspiration arising from understanding the pros and cons are thus the first ally that we call to mind and depend upon when setting out to achieve our goals and wishes.

Tenpa, the second ally, means steadfastness. With tenpa, Shantideva introduces three types of "pride." Usually pride is something to abandon, but in this case we learn to skillfully activate various forms of positive pride, or self-confidence, as a means of support in order to see our aspirations through to the end.

We will continue discussing these three types of positive pride in detail later in the text, but briefly, the three types of positive pride are in regard to the action or task itself, our ability to accomplish that task or aspiration, and overcoming obstacles along the way. In other words, it is knowing, *I can do this; I have the ability to do so; and I will overcome any obstacles that arise.* This kind of pride or self-confidence remedies lethargy and laziness, particularly when these stem from low self-esteem or self-disparagement. Having faced challenges in the past and overcome them, our sense of our ability and the success of our effort stays with us. Should we have to face different sorts of challenges going forward, it is still "us" facing a challenge, meaning, we know we have the ability to overcome whatever arises. Our sense of strength and confidence thus becomes stabler and more steadfast. That is the essence of tenpa.

Gawa means joy and is the third ally. Here we cultivate the conscious ability to take joy in our work, in an activity, or in whatever we are doing. This simply means being present and allowing ourselves to enjoy what we are doing while we are doing it. When we enjoy what we are doing in the moment, we want to keep doing that thing. We can also cultivate further joy by contemplating the outcome we are aiming for.

The fourth ally is dorwa, which means learning moderation. Here we begin to understand the importance of pacing ourselves. This can be learning to take short breaks, for instance, so that we may refresh ourselves and not become exhausted or burned out. When things become too difficult or we are too tired to continue, we sometimes need to retire for a bit to preserve our strength, interest, and enthusiasm. Moderating our efforts and resting when needed are important aspects of diligence practice. We consciously give ourselves time to rejuvenate so that we can keep going for the long run. If we burn out doing something for too long or with too much exertion or intensity, we are generally less inclined to reengage with that activity later. Before that happens, before we get burned out and overly fatigued, we must learn to take short breaks or retire for a bit and rest. This is what is meant by relinquishment or moderation.

In addition to the four allies, the two strengths, which Shantideva will cover in detail later in the verses, further enhance our joyful exertion. The two strengths help us to apply ourselves earnestly and become the master of ourselves in any endeavor. Up until this point, the verses help us to cultivate self-awareness so that we can identify laziness in our experience, explore the obstacles and challenges we face when setting out to achieve something, examine the various faces of our neuroses that are sure to arise, and exhort ourselves to think things through.

The first part of the Diligence chapter helps us to clarify what we want to abandon. The second part is about what we want to adopt—namely, the four allies and the two strengths. Wherever we sense resistance, laziness, or avoidance, we can call upon the four allies and the two strengths to help us find our way through to the completion of our endeavor. The four allies and the two strengths are what we cultivate as a support to accomplish our goals and aspirations, while abandoning the three kinds of laziness. As an illustrative exercise let's take the four allies and the two strengths into an example most of us can relate to: learning how to drive.

When we first begin to think about learning how to drive, most of us look forward to the experience and want to learn. Many reasons propel us to pursue this skill. There are great benefits to learning how to drive and lots of likely problems if we don't. Carefully thinking through these pros and cons, we feel inspired to acquire the knowledge and experience of driving.

As we begin to prepare, we may feel a bit anxious or disheartened, thinking, *It will be hard to drive on the highway. All the cars are going so fast. There are so many semitrucks. It is dangerous. How will I know what to make of all the signs and lights and lines? I might become overwhelmed and make a mistake!* Many people feel such things when they first learn to drive. If we lend these thoughts weight and give up whenever we think or feel such things, we will become discouraged and stuck. Instead, we need some resolve and a can-do attitude, and then we must think to ourselves, *Countless people have learned to drive, why not me?* We need to rouse this kind of oomph in the face of our anxiety and insecurity.

As we learn the rules, engage and apply ourselves, practice and remain consistent, we begin to relax and notice that we enjoy learning how to drive. We start to sense the freedom and independence that driving brings. Of course, we don't try to learn everything in one day. First we learn one thing well, like how to operate the car. Then we learn what the lines and signs mean, and step-by-step we build our knowledge and experience with each day of practice. If it becomes too challenging, we know we can take a break and come back when we are ready to absorb more information.

Driving is something we learn to make life more convenient, but it can also involve life-and-death situations for ourselves and everyone else on the road. Car accidents happen all the time. Applying ourselves, slowly adding to our knowledge, learning safe habits, and practicing with mindfulness are how we become a safe driver. We can see how each of the four allies is included here: First, we aspired to learn and looked in that direction. We applied ourselves with consistent, steadfast self-confidence and overcame our anxieties and challenges. We enjoyed the process and the experience of learning to drive. And when we became overwhelmed or tired, we took breaks to rest and rejuvenate so that we could come back fresh for another round.

Adding the two strengths to this, we consider our overall motivation to take on the task of learning to drive. With the first strength, earnest application, or lhur langwa, we rely upon our mindfulness and vigilant introspection—bakyö and shézhin—throughout the process of applying the four allies. Earnest application refers to our approach—our mindful attentiveness and introspection while employing the four allies.

The second strength is the perfection of that skill through familiarization, which allows us to exert control in the way we wish. This is wangdu jawa. In the example of learning how to drive, as we become more experienced and proficient through doing it over and over again and integrating it into our lives, driving becomes effortless. Soon we become a good driver, cruising down the highway at 75 mph while holding a conversation, drinking our coffee, listening to the news or music, and humming along while passing huge semis.

In reality, nothing has changed. The risks and dangers are all the same. We have simply become familiar with them and refined our skills through experience, overcoming obstacles, and consistent practice. We have learned how to avoid danger and proceed in a way that safely gets us where we wish to go—not just once, but many times a day. This is wangdu jawa—familiarizing and perfecting a skill until it becomes second nature, and we are the master of ourselves while engaging in that skill.

The two strengths can be summed up as, first, embracing the task, lhur langwa, and second, perfecting it, wangdu jawa. This is how we accomplish anything in life—learning to walk as a baby, learning to read or play the piano, learning to practice the spiritual path, becoming a doctor, or learning how to drive.

17

ASPIRATION

An Exercise of Choice

In verses 33–67, Shantideva explains the four allies in detail. We begin with möpa, or aspiration, which is covered in verses 33–46.

33
The boundless evils of myself and others—
I must bring them all to nothing,
Even though a single of these ills
May take unnumbered ages to exhaust!

34
And if I find within myself
No sign that faults are even starting to be cleansed,
Why does my heart not burst asunder,
Destined as I am for boundless pain?

35
Good qualities for my and others' sake,
Though they be many, I must now accomplish,
Even though for each of them
I must endeavor for unnumbered ages.

36

Acquaintance I have never gained
With even part of such great qualities.
It is indeed amazing that I render meaningless
This life that somehow I have gained.

Anything we wish to accomplish begins with aspiration, or möpa, the first ally. Clarifying our aspirations and our intentions is an exercise of our agency or choice. We are actively involved here, directing things with our mind and intention, not only in the beginning but every step of the way. We can't sit back and think that it should all happen on its own and that if it doesn't happen that way, then something is not working. We must be present with an active sense of choice at each stage of the process. This is the case with the spiritual path, as well as any other meaningful endeavor we wish to engage in.

Self-inspiration is a result of clarifying our intention through weighing pros and cons. Human beings are gifted with the ability to think, assess, and discern. One of the greatest aspects of our thinking process is being able to put things into perspective. Without the perspective and self-inspiration that arise from clarifying our intention by weighing pros and cons, we are left to our reactive emotions and the preferences of the self.

I want to be clear: There is absolutely nothing wrong with experiencing feelings and emotions, whatever they may be. But we must also be free to exercise intelligent discernment, lest our various states of mind and emotions take over and end up dictating our life. As mentioned earlier, emotions are like smoke that arises from our thoughts, which are like fire. These thoughts usually arise automatically in reference to our unquestioned belief in a self, the ensuing clinging to that self, and the tendencies to cherish or protect the self. That is how we operate until we learn that there is another way.

As we well know, our mind and thoughts can be fickle. We can, for instance, start a project, make it part way through, then get bored or anxious, and think to ourselves, *I have done enough. In fact, I have done plenty. Why do I need to do more? Actually, I don't know why I started this in the first place.* For an important task, something that has the potential to bring immense benefit, we must be ready to put in effort and be steadfast. We can't allow our fickle thoughts and feelings of fatigue or boredom to take over and make us give up so easily. That is childish. Getting a medical degree, for instance, takes effort, aspiration, steadfastness, and confidence over an extended period of time. Everyone who earns an MD has to work just as hard as all the MDs of the past in order to receive that degree. No one can declare that they are a special case and deserve a degree after only a year or two of medical school.

When we feel tired and disconnected, like we want to give up, or when we become anxious and start thinking of other things we might want to do instead of seeing our goal through, we must take a moment, turn inward, and allow time for self-reflection. Imagine seeing your goal through, and also imagine what will happen if you do not. Picture yourself giving in to your laziness, procrastination, and distraction, considering where each of these scenarios lead and how you will feel about that in the end.

Without using our mind and its power of discernment, we can hardly expect things to simply fall into place. So we should honestly ask ourselves: *What is our deeper motivation and intention? And what is our aspiration?* Only when we get down to contemplating such questions do we gain the clarity and space to inspire ourselves to move forward. This is how we discern which direction to take and the steps needed to get there. This is also how we discover the power of joyful exertion, tsöndru or diligence. Otherwise we are just dabbling, trying out a dispensable hobby, and on that course we ultimately achieve nothing.

As aspiring bodhisattvas on the path, Shantideva reminds us we aim to attain enlightenment for the benefit of all sentient beings. We have already lived countless lives, lacking any constructive direction through which to purify our obscurations or find genuine freedom, fulfillment, and joy. Remembering that this is the path that the buddhas and bodhisattvas traversed and not simply slumping into despair, self-loathing, or a "couldn't care less" attitude encourage us to keep going and not give up. Despairing and giving up are strategies of avoidance that arise from habitual tendencies to wallow in self-pity or simply numb out through laziness and dudzi activities. We never feel good after going down that road. So we rouse ourselves, remembering how the buddhas and bodhisattvas conducted themselves. We rouse ourselves by contrasting what we have done so far with what they have done. We do this, not to beat ourselves up, but as a means of exercising our choice, of inspiring and challenging ourselves, knowing with confidence that those who imitate best, act best.

Genuine fulfillment and freedom result from purifying our self-centered mindset and its neurosis. If freedom, fulfillment, and joy are what we wish for, then we must summon our effort and use our intelligent discernment, following in the footsteps of those who have gone before us. We must do all we can, give it our best, and courageously confront and purify our obscurations one by one. As an aspiring bodhisattva, we don't do this for our sake alone. Our aspiration and intention are to awaken ourselves for the sake of all humanity, all living beings, so that we can be of genuine benefit to them. This is why we tread the bodhisattva path and seek liberation. This gives our effort, diligence, aspiration, and self-confidence that much more weight and meaning. This all amounts to a great source of self-inspiration and propels us forward in a positive direction.

TWO FIELDS OF ACTIVITY: BUDDHAS AND SENTIENT BEINGS

37

Offerings to the Buddhas I have never made;
No feasts were ever held through my donations;
No works have I accomplished for the Teachings;
The wishes of the poor I left unsatisfied.

38

I have not saved the frightened from their fear;
The wretched I have not consoled.
My mother's pain, her womb's discomfort:
These alone are my accomplishments.

In the Buddhadharma there are two "fields" of activity: the Three Jewels and sentient beings. We make offerings to the Three Jewels or the buddhas and bodhisattvas, not because they need those offerings, but as a means of accumulating merit and purifying our own obscurations. Thanks to the aspirations of the buddhas and bodhisattvas in the past, along with their own tremendous gathering of past merit, when we connect with them through our devotion and gratitude for their activity and make heartfelt offerings, we also connect to their merit and aspirations. That connection has the power to shift things for us.

We can think of devotion as a pure form of appreciation—gratitude for the fact that such beings exist in the world and that we have a connection to their wisdom. Such appreciation and respect create an opening in our hearts that then allows that connection to grow. Fostering respectful appreciation for the Buddha, Dharma, and noble Sangha of bodhisattvas accumulates merit because the Three Jewels are the embodiment of wisdom. All goodness in the world comes from wisdom, never from ignorance and delusion. Dharma is wisdom, and wisdom is Dharma. The noble Sangha of bodhisattvas is the holder of that wisdom, and the Buddha is the teacher of that wisdom.

In these verses, Shantideva encourages us to reflect and ask ourselves, *What have I personally done to earn merit and practice virtue? Have I served the noble Sangha or worked to preserve and practice the Dharma? What other paramita practices have I engaged in for the benefit of beings? How have I made this life meaningful?*

If we recognize that we have done something significant or beneficial, how did we do that? Was it with pure motivation? With the altruism of aspiration bodhichitta? Did we dedicate the merit in the end so that our effort and aspirations were directed to bear their intended fruit? If we did well, then we want to acknowledge that and rejoice. If we can fully rejoice, we will likely notice the fulfillment, joy, and peace that such deeds bring to our own heart and mind and naturally feel inspired to do more.

It is not an ego trip to rejoice in one's own positive deeds, as long as we are free of making a claim for the self—as if *I* have done this and *I* have done that, it is all about *my* role, all about *me, me, me*. If thoughts or feelings arise to claim one's good deeds for the self—for the ego—that is initially OK. This happens. Spontaneously arising thoughts and feelings cannot be controlled, and controlling them is not the point. What we can do, however, is self-reflect and notice if the ego is grasping to make a claim, to puff itself up, or to assert some superiority. Knowing full well that the ego's claim does not help us, we can let go with humor and gentleness. We can remember that all beings without exception are endowed with Buddha nature or basic goodness. Our Buddha nature does not need the claim of the ego in order to operate and to benefit beings. In fact, when ego's claim moves in and takes over, it generally ends up ruining everything.

We want to achieve liberation, enlightenment, and lasting happiness and peace. Everything we do, therefore, must eventually be processed through the knowledge and practice of letting go of the self and replacing it with love and altruism for all beings, while continuing to do whatever it is that we are doing. Even though all of us as sentient beings are naturally endowed with Buddha nature and basic goodness, in order to pull away the veils that obscure that Buddha nature and hinder our progress, we must continue to gather merit and wisdom and exert ourselves in the paramita practices. This is why we exercise our virtue and gather merit in relation to the field of the Three Jewels.

The other field of activity as aspiring bodhisattvas is sentient beings. Sentient beings are just as important to us as the Three Jewels. It is impossible to practice the paramitas, accumulate merit, or progress on the path without sentient beings. There is no perfection of generosity, moral discipline, or patience without the presence of other sentient beings. If there were no beings to be generous toward and help, how would we practice the paramita of generosity, or *dana* in Sanskrit? If there were no beings to refrain from harming and to benefit instead, how would we practice the paramita of moral discipline, or *shila*? If no one provoked or irritated us, what opportunity would we have to work on the paramita of patience, or *ksanti*? And without working on these paramitas, we would have nothing to inspire our practice of diligence, or virya. So while the paramitas of concentration or *dhyana* and wisdom or *prajna* are vitally important to the development of our inner path, the relative paramitas that depend on sentient beings are equally important in developing our loving kindness and compassion and ultimately showing us where we are on the path and in our life.

Holding deep appreciation—devotion even—toward sentient beings and engaging with loving kindness and compassion, especially when we are challenged, accumulates great waves of merit and wisdom and cleanses our own mind stream. As a reminder, we can ask ourselves, *Have I been generous and helped those in need, poor people, sick people, elders, or those who are helpless, like animals or insects? In particular, have I been able to help my own parents, or those who have raised me, with their needs? Have I done what I can to help them whenever I could? Did I help when the opportunity presented itself? Was I able to come out of myself and be there for those outside of "me and mine"? Have I protected and given refuge to beings whose lives were threatened?* We must strive to engage in altruistic activities and intentions, free of self-serving motives, and use our relationships and interactions with others as a mirror to see ourselves and penetrate our most hidden hang-ups, rather than point out the faults of others.

If we have engaged in virtuous deeds and aspirations with an altruistic mind, we should rejoice and let that reflection inspire us to do more. If not, then we want to look into our self-investment or the sense of self-congratulation and pride. Laying that bare helps us to let go of the ego that is endlessly hungry to be at the center of everything. Consciously letting go of our self-centeredness allows our heart to be clean and free the next time around. Letting go of the ego and rejoicing in virtue—our own deeds and those of others—not only bring great meaning to our lives but inspire tremendous joy as well.

If we find that we have not practiced any of the paramitas of generosity, moral discipline, patience, diligence, meditation, and wisdom, nor made offerings to the Three Jewels, then we want to openly and nonjudgmentally ask ourselves why. *While the opportunity presented itself, when someone needed my help or was asking for my assistance, and I could have done something but didn't, why was that? Even while believing in helping others, what held me back? What prevented me from extending myself and benefiting another?*

Apart from the storyline, it is important to touch base with our tightness and sense of self-justification and self-protection. It is important to sit with that, to let ourselves simmer in the raw feeling of discomfort that this kind of frank self-examination can provoke. This is not a futile exercise, nor is it about judging, beating up, or being hard on ourselves. We must take care not to let ourselves slip into thought patterns of "bad me" or, on the other hand, make excuses for ourselves. Both of these extremes are merely an avoidance of the temporary discomfort of sitting honestly with ourselves. Instead, we allow ourselves to simmer in that discomfort for a bit. Sitting openly and honestly in the middle, without falling into either extreme, is how we walk the fine line of genuine self-reflection, which allows wisdom to arise from within. This is how we learn from our shortfalls and make progress.

The Three Jewels and sentient beings are thus equally important as fields of activity and engagement on the path, and we must remember to cultivate devotion and appreciation toward both. We can ponder this further, as Shantideva does, by considering: *My mother carried me for nine months—not outside of her body, but inside of her abdomen, feeding me from her own flesh and blood. Then she gave birth to me, which caused her tremendous pain, even posing a risk to her own life. How can I waste all her effort? Her time, care, love, and hardship spent in bringing me into the world—will it amount to something meaningful and beneficial, or will I stay self-concerned and self-focused, ignoring the suffering of other sentient beings, those who are in need right in front of me?*

We all tend to take things for granted in life. We forget to acknowledge the factors that contribute to our well-being and what we have in our lives. We tend to assume that things are simply how they should be or it is all our own achievement, all our own genius and effort. Nothing, however, could be further from the truth.

Everything we are and have is due to the kindness of others, especially our own mothers, along with our fathers and other parental figures, teachers, guides, and friends. It is helpful to acknowledge this, especially when we find ourselves self-absorbed and oblivious to what is happening around us. All the suffering we have ever experienced or ever will experience in samsara comes from our past negative deeds, meaning actions spurred by our afflictive emotions, rooted in our self-at-the-center-of-the-universe mindset. So rather than trying to avert all kinds of things from the outside, we want to learn to work with our own mind and use whatever is arising as a means to purify our self-centeredness and negative deeds.

We absolutely can transform our negative states into positive ones—that is the nature of karma and dependent origination. Nothing is set in stone. It may be that we experience suffering in this life—the result of past negative deeds—but how we relate to what is arising now is what makes all the difference. We presently have choices and can influence the unfolding outcome of our life and deeds in a positive direction. This is a vital point. Karma, or cause and effect, is not predestined. It all depends on how we engage our mind in the present moment, or shortly afterward if a situation happens to be too intense in the moment. It all depends on how we relate to what arises.

18

DEDICATING THE MERIT

All goodness in the world, every pleasurable or happy experience, such as feeling supported by loved ones and enjoying positive conditions, meeting the spiritual path and an authentic guide—all of this comes from our past virtuous deeds. And especially in finding conditions for following a genuine spiritual path of liberation, such things don't just spring up all by themselves. They come from our own aspirations and altruistic deeds in the past.

It is helpful to note the critical role that dedicating the merit plays for us. Positive deeds can bear fruit once or continually, depending on how we direct the merit, or energy, of those deeds. If we want to reinvest the energy of our positive deeds and allow that energy to grow in order to support us now and in the future, then we must learn to dedicate our merit toward greater causes.

The greatest cause—which covers all positive causes—is the benefit and ultimate enlightenment of all sentient beings. We are also included in this dedication. In fact, even though our motivation is for the benefit of all sentient beings, as a person with a mind dedicated to such an outcome, we are the ones who benefit first and foremost. This is just the way things work. As I have mentioned, His Holiness the Dalai Lama often jokes that, if you want to be happy, the best way is to be a bodhisattva—to dedicate your life to the benefit of all living beings. On that course, we are always sustained, always buoyant, always joyful. So, if happiness, joy, and fulfillment are what we wish for, then the right course of action is to engage in positive, altruistic deeds dedicated to the benefit of all sentient beings. In this way, even if we encounter great suffering and misfortune, that is not all that is going on. We have an inner path and an inner practice of altruism that changes how we see and respond to things.

This is how we understand and relate to the practice of virtue and to dedicating the merit of such virtue. Virtue is not accumulated by physical or verbal deeds alone. The presence and intention of the mind must be there for the accumulation of virtue or nonvirtue, merit or demerit, to occur. Machines and robots can do good deeds and help beings, but they do not accumulate merit because they do not have a mind. Machines and AI can mimic the functions of the mind, sometimes extremely well. But because they are not sentient—meaning primordially endowed with a mind that feels pain and pleasure, suffering and happiness—there is no accumulation or loss of merit through virtuous or harmful deeds.

The mind that is seated in this present body for the time being, motivating us to engage in physical and verbal acts with intention and aspiration, is the one that creates karma, the one that accumulates virtue and merit—or the opposite. This present physical body will, at some point, be left behind. Speech will likewise cease with the cessation of the body. The mind that sows the seed and reaps the fruit—both positive and negative—will continue, propelled by karma, and migrate into a newly formed physical body with its accompanying faculties.

The mind, therefore, is the most important factor to determine the direction and results of our deeds. Once again, the most important factor in determining the state of our mind is our motivation. If our motivation is self-centered, then our actions and speech bring little positive result, particularly for ourselves. If our mind and our motivation are rooted in altruism, aimed at the benefit of beings as a whole—humanity and all sentient beings as one universal self—then the actions and speech ensuing from that state of mind have much more positive power and weight, both presently and in the long run. This positive energy changes the environment of our own being and the environment around us. We can affect our immediate surroundings when we practice the four immeasurables with a genuine, altruistic heart. This is a powerful energy to put out into the world.

The best, and only, place to start our practice, particularly the practice of the four immeasurables, is right where we are. We must be honest about our present motivation and intention and not try to fool anyone, especially ourselves. This honesty brings us down to earth, where we have solid ground on which to stand, and then walk forward, one step at a time.

39
My failure to aspire to Dharma
Now and in the past
Has brought me to my present dereliction.
Who therefore would spurn such aspiration?

40
Aspiration, so the Sage asserted,
Is the root of every kind of virtue.
Aspiration's root in turn
Is constant meditation on the fruits of action.

If we are not motivated to practice the Dharma, or more precisely, to observe the natural laws of cause and effect, and yet still want happiness in this life and beyond, we must think to ourselves in this way: *I have wandered in the suffering of samsara all this time, trying this and trying that, wishing to attain well-being and fulfillment. The approaches I've tried have failed to achieve my goal in any lasting or significant way. If I keep doing the same thing while expecting a different outcome, how will that ever change things?* Shantideva is encouraging us to rely upon the first ally of aspiration, using our intelligence and self-reflection to move beyond the approaches we have taken thus far. Knowing that the Buddha said that all goodness comes from aspiring to a genuinely altruistic motivation, we can weigh the pros and cons, the benefits and losses of our actions, and we can aspire to do our best to connect our actions with our intentions, understanding that the outcome of our deeds depends on how we see our aspirations through.

After all, how long do we want to wander? Even if we obtain outer wealth or success, we must always assess what is happening within, in our mind and heart, as that is what we will be left with in the end. Genuinely beneficial motivation and aspiration come from objectively observing or weighing the benefits and losses of how we proceed and ultimately assessing what is at stake. In these verses, Shantideva is rhetorically asking, who in their right mind would reject making such altruistic aspirations, backed up by one's own intelligence and discernment?

41
The body's pains, anxieties of mind,
And all my fears of various kinds,
To be deprived of what I want—
Such is the harvest of my sinful deeds.

42
But if my acts are good, sincerely intended,
Then no matter where I turn my steps,
The merit gained will honor me
With its resulting benefits.

43
But if, through seeking happiness, my deeds are wrong,
No matter where I turn my steps,
The knives of misery will cut me down,
The wage and retribution of a sinful life.

All experiences are a result of our actions, positive or negative, which in turn are driven by our positive or negative motivations. Our fears and the suffering we experience in samsara generally come from self-centeredness and negativity, while the pleasures and enjoyments in life come from positive and virtuous actions and intentions. All that we experience comes down to our own motivation: how we position our mindset—toward altruism or toward self-centered aims. Reflecting on how samsara is full of suffering, without becoming discouraged, we can allow ourselves to be moved and inspired to mature our wisdom mind. After all, here we are, connected to the path of the Buddha's wisdom mind. If we take that for granted or waste this chance to benefit ourselves and others due to sheer distraction, laziness, or arrogance, it may be hard to meet such an opportunity again. Thinking of the suffering of beings here on earth and in the lower realms and understanding what is at stake motivate us to mature our own wisdom and the potential of our mind right away.

19

CONSIDERING AN UNDERSTANDING OF REBIRTH

44

Through virtue I will rest within the cool heart of a fragrant
    spreading lotus,
With splendor nurtured by the sweet words of the Conqueror.
Then from the lotus opened in the Sage's light, in supreme form
    I will arise
To dwell, the blissful Buddha's heir, in presence of Victorious
    Ones.

No matter how we look at it, this life will be over soon. We don't know
how or when it will end, but that end will most certainly come. We thus
want to focus our mind and aim to continue our path after this present
life ends. We aspire to be reborn in circumstances where we may meet
the Dharma, receive teachings, and allow that wisdom to open the lotus petals of our heart so that we may awaken and mature our mind
for the benefit of all beings. In essence, we want to continue our path
until complete enlightenment. For some people this may be difficult to
fathom or even to feel open to. Our world has become quite agnostic
and nihilistic. In our modern culture, however, supported by an almost

absolute faith in science and technology, we may have thrown the baby out with the bathwater.

Open, intelligent critical thinking and analysis are always encouraged in the Buddhist path. The faith we have in what can be proven in science, with its attempted objectivity and need for findings to be seen to be believed, doubtlessly has value. But leaning too heavily on this approach can push aside, or in some cases altogether reject, faith in what we can't always see, in the spiritual side of our mind or what may happen after we leave this particular existence. This is unfortunate. Ironically, many of us don't seem interested in applying the same critical eye that we have apparently used to analyze spiritual faith, the mind stream, rebirth, and the experiences of our inner life to what we are told by science and technology.

It is not that we must unquestioningly believe in rebirth, but we can at least be open to the thoughts and observations of great minds. What evidence do we have, after all, that our mind stream will *not* continue or that we will *not* be reborn once we leave this life? We experience our mind stream continuing from day into night, into and out of dream states, into the unconscious, and back to conscious daytime experiences—all from the moment of taking up residence in this particular body to its very last breath. This is our own direct experience. What evidence do we have that our experience of our mind stream will stop or has ever stopped? If our physical body, which seems so solid and real, breaks apart into countless atoms, and those atoms then reconstitute themselves into different forms in a constant flow of regeneration, why would this not be possible with our own mind stream? (Of course, not in the sense of an identity of the self, but with the mind and its stream of consciousness.)

Based on personal evidence, we can all verify that our mind stream is experienced. But can we pinpoint our mind stream, or put it in a box and say, "Here it is!"? Where are the boundaries of our mind? Right now, where does the mind begin, and where does it end? Can we locate that? Isn't it always changing, unfolding, experiencing? If something like the atoms that constitute our body morph and change, taking on new form—all of which is scientifically established—why not the mind? Why can't the mind, so ephemeral when compared to the body, also continue once it separates from the body? A better question might be: what would make it *not* continue? These are some interesting points to openly consider.

This is not about convincing anyone of anything. I would, however, appeal to our deeper intelligence not to close down into nihilism, which is merely another extreme, another belief that we have taken for granted and accepted because it is popularly accepted, particularly in this day and age. In reality, nihilism is ego's last stand, its final escape route in hopes of avoiding pain. Therefore, such a view or reaction is not coming from a negative place. It is simply more convenient for the ego to think and believe that it all just ends, that our mind dries up like a puddle of water when we die, and thus that nothing really matters in the end. Like its extreme counterpart eternalism, which holds to some form of an eternal self forever existing in the hereafter, nihilism is, ultimately, a way for the ego to escape taking responsibility for its actions.

Logically speaking, how can we take a single chapter out of a book and not accept that there are other chapters before or after? It is not sensible. This would suggest that, in such an arbitrarily chosen slice of time, there is no cause for anything that is presently happening here and now and no cause for anything that might happen in the future. Nihilism, therefore, is an emotional preference in attempting to escape causal effects or accountability. Chandrakirti said in the *Introduction to the Middle Way*, "In the absolute, everything is beyond cause and effect. But in our relative world of karma, in the functioning of everything we all experience, cause and effect are very ordered and precise, based on dependent origination. Everything in our relative experience arises from causes and conditions, and everything regenerates and continues. The position that rejects and denies this is simplistic, not worthy of genuine philosophical discussion." Simply stating that one does not "believe" in anything after this life is, therefore, also quite simplistic.

If everything is merely composed of inanimate elements and consciousness is just a by-product of such elements or chemical reactions, which ceases to exist when the body does, how do we explain the experience of our self-cognizant mind stream occurring in this present life? If it has been produced in this present life of ours, why would it not be produced again, if the right causes and conditions are present? Not with the identity of the self that we currently have and cling to as "me," but the naked mind stream and its innate awareness, which holds the relative seeds of cause and effect. Again, these are all important points to openly ponder. At the very least, we should have the intelligence to leave the question open and the humility to respect the great minds who have deeply and thoroughly studied these topics and gained realization.

The extreme views of eternalism and nihilism are not new inventions—they have been around since the dawn of human attempts to understand how and why the world functions as it does. Both approaches cling to a particular view in order to explain how cause and effect function, yet both lack the subtlety and simplicity of dependent origination and emptiness or the Middle Way.

Lacking the hearing wisdom of the Buddha's teachings on the Middle Way, we feel that we have no alternative but to start grasping at one possible explanation after another. This is not necessary and only creates more confusion for ourselves. These days there are many texts available, translated into every spoken language, which clearly elucidate the Buddha's teachings on emptiness and dependent origination. If we have questions about the nature of reality, rebirth, and how the mind functions, we should not be idle but rather study and contemplate these teachings to our satisfaction.

Of course, everyone is free to believe what they wish. The Buddha's view of the Middle Way, however, gives us an understanding beyond this fleeting present life. As the chapter of this life closes and the next one begins, these teachings offer a virtuous and inspiring motivation to continue with the next chapter and then the next chapter and then the next. Understanding and having faith in the Middle Way gives our heart strength and clarity to face the transitions ahead, as well as whatever challenges may come during that time and beyond. Especially regarding the practice of virtue and the bodhisattva's path of awakening, understanding and having faith in these give us much to look forward to—not as a possession of the "self" or ego, but as a fruition of our merit, dedicated to the benefit of others.

Without such faith, we can succumb to depression and hopelessness, especially as we approach death. This is not necessary. If we have lived a good and virtuous life, have helped others, and have been kind and altruistic, we can use all that energy as momentum to carry us forward and continue on, particularly if we have a spiritual path and direction. And if we have not been virtuous, we can still change. We can confess our self-centeredness and stop acting in ways that do not support us. It is never too late for such purification and a change of our ways. As it is said, "There is no goodness in 'sin' or harmful deeds—but the one good thing about such deeds is that they can be confessed and purified." Nihilism does none of this. It is just nihilism and leaves us in a bleak, flat state of mind. This is why the Indian master Nagarjuna said in the *Garland of Jewels*, "Eternalists go up, nihilists go down, while the Middle Way finds liberation."

All of this is to say that the logic and reason behind nihilism and eternalism should be thoroughly explored. We want to be open to exploring the logic of our emotions, lest we become enslaved to our reactive mind. Using nihilism as an excuse to avoid being accountable for one's actions ultimately only produces tyrants and tyranny.

45
Or else as wages of my many sins, my skin completely flayed, I
    shall be utterly brought low
By creatures of the Lord of Death, who on my body pour a
    liquid bronze all melted in the dreadful blaze.
And pierced by burning swords and knives, my flesh
Dismembered in a hundred parts will fall upon the white-hot
    iron ground.

Here Shantideva is weighing the advantages of practicing bodhichitta versus following the ego and the ignorant, self-centered mind. The result of following our ego is confusion and suffering, now and in the future. The result of practicing bodhichitta is liberation, happiness, and well-being for oneself and others. This is how Shantideva motivates himself to take up the practice of bodhichitta and leave behind his allegiance to ego and the self-centered mindset of ignorance.

46

Therefore I will aspire and tend to virtue,
And steep myself in it with great devotion.
And with the method stated in the *Vajradhvaja*,
I will train in confident assurance.

Shantideva sums up the first of the four allies—möpa, or aspiration—
by referencing the Vajra Banner sutra, which states, "Just as the sun,
without concern for clouds or fog, shines and lights up the whole
world, bringing warmth and benefit to all, free of despondency or lack
of reach, likewise, bodhisattvas strive to take birth wherever they can
be of benefit, free of despondency, and with great self-confidence to
benefit beings through the practice of bodhichitta." Just as the sun remains independent, yet benefits all who are touched by its light rays and
warmth, likewise bodhisattvas dive into the ocean of samsara to benefit
beings, yet remain untouched by the dense delusion of ignorance.

20

STARTING SMALL AND FINISHING WHAT WE START

In verses 47–62, Shantideva covers the second ally of steadfastness through three kinds of self-confidence:

47

Let me first consider my reserves—
To start or not to start accordingly.
It might be better not to start,
But once begun, I should not then withdraw.

Here, Shantideva gets down to the business of practicality. The whole of the Buddhist path is, in fact, extremely practical and realistic. Once we have considered all the pros and cons, have established our motivation, and inspired ourselves to altruistic intentions and the Middle Way, we must then take a hard look at our circumstances and our state of mind.

Before engaging in any significant act, we should first carefully analyze whether it is worthwhile. If we see the benefit of how such an act will support our deeper aspirations and the work we must do to accomplish those aspirations, then the second thing is to analyze whether such an act is within our means to accomplish. Shantideva encourages us to analyze ahead of time and honestly assess whether or not we can see something through before we commit. This analysis is not coming from self-centeredness. It is meant to realistically de-termine our chances of success. It is said that noble ones do not make promises lightly or frequently, but once committed to something, they see it through to the end.

If we see that something is not within our means to accomplish, even if it is a positive deed, we should hold back for the time being and not proceed. We should wait until circumstances shift and allow us a way forward. If we see that we can proceed, however, then we should do so. If we can help, if we can do something, if the path is clear, then we most certainly want to proceed. To hold back then would be a mistake.

Furthermore, once we start something significant, we should not drop out; we should follow it through to completion. If we start some-thing and don't finish it, that can become a habit, which damages our self-esteem and dims our general outlook on life. The depression that afflicts many people often arises from the habit of starting something and then dropping out—not seeing things through to a conclusion. This approach never yields much fruit and only exhausts us and makes us lose confidence. This is why we must take care to examine whether we are prepared to complete a task before we begin it. Remember that habits are created in four ways: repetition, periodic intensity, lack of a counter-agent, and availability of the field. These four aspects apply to positive and harmful habits alike, so we want to use them to our advantage.

48
For if I do such things, the pattern will return
In later lives, and sin and pain will grow.
And other actions will be left undone
Or else will bear a meager fruit.

The habit of starting things and not finishing them can be hard to break. It is important, therefore, to assess and respect our capability, and not overshoot it. If we want to do something, but don't feel ready or capa-ble, it does not mean that we must abandon it altogether. Instead, we can put our effort into making aspirations that our circumstances will shift, so that we may come to see a pathway forward. Making aspirations like this, especially when we want to do something but know that it is presently beyond us, is a powerful way to keep moving forward in the direction we wish to go.

It is better to start small and successfully complete tasks that are manageable, than to take on monumental goals and set impossibly high standards for ourselves. If we start small and succeed in seeing things through, we set a force in motion that develops a pattern, and that helps us take on more as the pattern and momentum build.

Small or big, the task itself is not the important thing. What is important is learning to see something through and developing the confidence that builds from doing something thoroughly. Finishing what we begin increases our strength and confidence and builds momentum. It leaves a positive imprint on our mind. This positive momentum and self-confidence thus help us accomplish our goals and aspirations, both in our worldly life and on the spiritual path.

It can be helpful to take an objective look at the world and contemplate how ordinary people work so hard—sometimes their whole life long—to achieve very little fruit or benefit. They spend days, weeks, months, and years exerting themselves without much rest. They face physical, emotional, mental, and financial struggles, enduring all manner of stresses just to scrape together a little means or establish a bit of conventional standing in life. If ordinary people in the world work so hard, how can we, while having a connection to a path of wisdom and compassion and a higher aspiration to be of benefit to others, just sit around and stew in our self-absorption and not rouse ourselves? If common folks can work so hard, we can also joyfully rouse ourselves to accomplish what we wish to do, starting small and proceeding step-by-step.

THREE KINDS OF POSITIVE PRIDE

49
Action, the afflictions, and ability:
Three things to which my pride should be directed.
"I will do this, I myself, alone!"
These words define my pride of action.

The teachings on how to generate self-confidence begin in earnest with verse 49. This verse defines three fields of self-confidence, or "pride," on which we want to focus:

1. **Action:** Once we have examined whether an aspiration or project is doable, we generate confidence to execute the work required. This confidence is in regard to the task or action itself.

2. **Ability:** Knowing what the aspiration or project requires in terms of action, we then generate a can-do attitude with confidence in our ability. We know that we are able and that we can develop further skills as we go. This can-do attitude is the confidence in our capability.

3. **Overcoming affliction:** No matter what challenges may arise as we proceed, we generate confidence to confront and overcome them one by one, knowing that we can see our aspiration or the project through.

Usually, we are discouraged from acting arrogant, prideful, or cocky. To a certain degree, even conventional society acknowledges the shortcomings of pride. But here, a certain kind of pride is actively encouraged. This kind of pride is not about being better than others, but rather a "can-do" mentality, an attitude of *I can do this!* and *Why not?* Such positive thinking is very useful in developing self-confidence. Here, it is not necessarily about getting things done on the outside, but more about getting things done within—meaning overcoming our own self-importance, ignorance, and self-doubt. We apply the "can-do, why not, of course" mentality, not as a way to show off to others, but as a means to overcome where we are stuck in ourselves.

The momentum of this approach increases as we first engage small, manageable things, and then we build slowly upon that habit. Once we have seen something through once, twice, and then a number of times, we gain confidence in our resourcefulness, and we know that we do not need to panic or close down when challenges arise. This is the kind of grounded self-confidence that emerges from starting small with positive energy. We can apply this to both our spiritual and conventional lives, but here we emphasize developing this approach in relation to getting to our meditation cushion, relating to our mind, and honestly reflecting on what is holding us back.

Self-confidence can have the guise of pride, but it is in fact a positive antidote. We use it against the neurosis that creeps in to tell us, *I can't do it. I can't overcome my attachment and my grasping and my habitual patterns. I can't overcome my anger, my reactiveness, or my judgments. I have messed up again and can't seem to overcome this.* Or we may be plagued by recurring thoughts that, *Others are so much better than me; they are special, blessed, gifted, wealthy, and so on, and I am not.*

The fact of the matter is that we are all essentially the same in our makeup as human beings. No matter how things appear on the outside, everyone struggles and triumphs in the same manner. Acknowledging this gives us room to apply ourselves and grow, not as something to show to others or to make a splash, but to become free, fulfilled, and at peace inside. Thus we use self-confidence to tell ourselves, *Yes, I can! I can overcome my attachments. I can overcome my destructive habits, my anger, my grasping, my ignorance—it is in my hands. I can face this, and I can do it! It might be difficult and I might fail a hundred or a thousand times, but I know that I can do this.*

This is our agency and choice speaking, guided by wisdom. This kind of positive pride is extremely helpful in our spiritual practice and in our day-to-day lives. It supports healthy self-confidence and is used against the neurosis that makes us think that we aren't good enough or that blames someone or something else for things not going as planned. This approach keeps us open and healthily self-secure, preventing us from shutting down into failure, self-disparagement, and laziness.

An important aspect of developing genuine self-confidence is learning to humbly accept that we are all essentially equal. There is no need to make ourselves big and others small or to make others big and ourselves small. There is no need to be dualistic in this way. True greatness lies not in how unique and special we can be, but in how ordinary, grounded, and humble we are. From this place we can look toward those who have done whatever it is that we also wish to do and have the confidence to know that we can do it as well. Of course, we must train ourselves, starting small and developing our strength and ability, and work on gathering the various causes and conditions to succeed, but, essentially, we know that we can. This is particularly so if we remember to remain down-to-earth and humble with the self-confidence that knows that we and others are, fundamentally, all the same.

Verses 50 and 51 are about cultivating self-confidence/pride in regard to the action or task itself.

50
Overpowered by their minds' afflictions,
Worldly folk are helpless to secure their happiness.
Compared with those who wander, I am able!
This therefore shall be my task.

Here, Shantideva encourages us to recognize our advantages, all the things we have on our side and in our favor, especially compared to so many who lack what we likely take for granted. We must remember that we have access to wisdom and means, and we have the interest, time, and ability to do the work at hand and to overcome our obscurations. We are not inanimate beings; we live, breathe, and evolve. We are on the path—"a work in progress"—and we can develop our potential toward enlightenment by continually gathering wisdom and skillful means.

It can be helpful to reflect and objectively compare ourselves to others, not as a way of establishing our superiority, but simply as a means to acknowledge and appreciate what we have and not take our connection to a genuine source of wisdom for granted. Many beings are helplessly caught in dire situations, snared by the noose of negative karma and conditions, and powerless to do anything but submit to those conditions. Others are simply lost in delusion or on the wrong track. Of course, we have much ground to cover on our path, but we have found the trailhead of wisdom. We have spotted the pathway leading out of the woods: we have a connection to the wisdom of

Dharma, which transcends what is normally available and valued in our conventional world.

Pride of action is essentially the pride of being on the bodhisattva path and appreciating our connection. Once again, this is not a pride of ego but one of self-confidence that knows that if fulfillment, joy, and freedom are what we wish for, then the bodhisattva path of considering self and others as equal, exchanging ourself and others, and eventually considering others as more important than our singular self—in short, learning to embrace the universal self that cares for all beings equally—is the right track. Positive pride in action arises from the knowledge that the bodhisattva path regards all sentient beings as equal to oneself. When we act from this place, we feel secure and grounded.

The bodhisattva's intention is completely focused on the happiness, freedom, and well-being of all sentient beings. That is why bodhisattvas can dedicate their body, possessions, and merit toward that aim with full confidence. Embracing this intention and taking pride or feeling secure in our actions stemming from bodhichitta are like planting a medicinal seed. If properly nurtured, that seed will grow a healthy medicinal root, and the medicinal leaves and fruits of that tree can bring benefit to many. The medicinal seed of tenderness can blossom and bear fruit as countless beneficial qualities, such as loving kindness, compassion, and all the activities of the six paramitas.

When it begins to sink in that all beings equally long for happiness and freedom from suffering just like us, we realize that there is no reason to focus only on the self. Why not focus on all beings? Why not adopt a bigger view of the universal self that embraces all sentient beings as equal to oneself? This deeply personal, internal shift is the seed of altruism, the medicinal seed of altruism and happiness. This tender seed gives birth to bodhichitta and brings forth fulfillment and joy for oneself and others.

If we are not yet convinced that our self-importance brings suffering for ourselves and all beings, then we have not yet reached the trailhead of the bodhisattva's path. We are still wandering around in the forest. Once we truly understand the pain that self-importance brings, we may still from time to time forget and find ourselves back in our habitual focus on the singular self. When we realize this, however, we don't feel lost or confused. We know what to do. We know that this is the moment to give rise to our pride of action, our pride of being a bodhisattva in training, and, particularly, our pride in the autonomous choice that we have made to discover our deepest potential.

If there is no confusion or lack of awareness, even if the habit of self-importance still remains, it is a very workable situation. When confusion and the habit exist together, however, that is another matter. Once we are clear that altruism is to be adopted and our self-centeredness abandoned, our habit may still linger for a while, even after we have gained such clarity. This is OK. We should not emphasize the fact that our habit is still there, giving it a lot of weight. That is not helpful or necessary. Instead, we want to emphasize our clarity and our autonomous choice of altruism over self-centeredness. Consciously aligning ourselves with that view gives us a tremendous advantage. From here we can proceed with confidence and simply let the habit slowly and naturally wear itself out.

51

When others give themselves to low behavior,
What shall be my stance in their regard?
In any case, I'll not be arrogant;
My best way is to give up such conceit.

The pride that Shantideva encourages is never at the expense of other beings, nor is it built upon comparing ourselves to others as a means to feel egotistically elated. It is meant to genuinely and humbly inspire us toward virtue. Here, we honestly acknowledge the difference between adopting a universal altruistic self based on bodhichitta versus the conventional approach—which we ourselves often habitually take—of "me first." From time to time, it is helpful to ask ourselves, *Where did all my suffering of the past come from? Where does it arise from now? Where did any kindness, goodness, or joy come from? How does anything that is experienced as genuinely positive arise?* This reflection helps us to maintain our perspective and not become confused or disoriented.

We should be particularly mindful when we notice ourselves becoming judgmental toward others. Judgment has a negative emotional charge to it—we can feel this charge, and so can others. Discernment, on the other hand, openly sees and assesses the best course without the negative charge of judgment. We may observe someone acting self-absorbed or in a selfish manner. Discerning that behavior is part of our critical intelligence, which we can also use to examine why they might be acting in such a way. But as soon as we cross over into judgment, we lapse into negativity, and that negativity is ours alone. Objectively distinguishing the bodhisattva's path from the "me first" approach is meant to inspire us to strive as a bodhisattva in training. Reflecting on how much beings strive for conventional fruits can inspire us to strive for the sake of the Dharma, to awaken ourselves for the benefit of all beings.

At Guna Norling, our Buddhist center in Brazil, the local fishermen arrive each morning by four o'clock to set up for the day. They sit out on the craggy outcrops in front of the center in the hot sun and gusting wind, casting their lines into the open ocean, catching one little fish after another. Some days they don't have much luck, and other days they do well. Looking at them already out there by the time I get up inspires me to get right to my *tun*, or meditation session. Observing their tenacity helps me rouse my own determination and self-confidence to get on with my practice. *If they can get out there before the sun comes up and sit there all day just to catch a pailful of fish,* I think to myself, *I should certainly be able to do my full morning session and dedicate the merit to them and their pails of fish.*

If we struggle to get up a little earlier to do our practice before having to attend to all the demanding affairs of the day, if we resist cultivating the three wisdoms and start to feel despondent, we should rouse our confidence with a can-do mentality and say to ourselves, *I can do this. I am fully capable and able.* We often just need a little extra oomph to remind ourselves that we can.

Verses 52–59 are about cultivating the second kind of self-confidence or pride with regard to one's abilities.

52
When they find a dying serpent,
Even crows behave like soaring eagles.
Therefore, if I'm weak and feeble-hearted,
Even little faults will strike and injure me.

If we act dead before we are dead, we set ourselves up to be attacked as if we were dead. If we succumb to the slightest challenge or hardship, if we lose our self-confidence or our oomph when we face obstacles, then we are like a dying serpent who, even though being pecked at while still alive, does nothing to defend itself. Ordinarily, a large snake would never be threatened by crows or attacked by other birds, but if it lies still, looking and acting dead, then even timid little birds will muster their nerve and start to attack as if they were fierce falcons or other birds of prey.

With this metaphor Shantideva is saying, if we give into our low self-esteem, if we slump into a "can't-do" mentality, then even small neuroses can become threatening and overwhelm us. When we give up on ourselves prematurely, obstacles pile up, and we feel more and more threatened and overwhelmed, afraid of even the smallest things. At some point there won't be a cocoon comfortable enough in which to hide. It will get worse and worse.

We cannot run away from our own shadow. Similarly, we cannot run from our own obstacles. If we try to run away from one obstacle, others will rise to challenge us. This is particularly true when relating to and working with our own mind. We must thus have self-confidence and rouse our positive pride, saying to ourselves, *I can handle this. I can do this. I can practice through my meditation session without distraction. I can finish what I started.*

We must have this predetermined mindset. Otherwise, if we promise a lot or promise but don't deliver on our promises—especially the promises we make to ourselves—we become a laughingstock and are written off by others as unreliable and not to be depended upon. This form of laziness sucks the life out of our self-confidence and self-worth. Even though we may accomplish many things on the outside, if we can't fulfill our inner commitments, we end up feeling internally split—as if we are one person on the outside and another on the inside. And if we can't keep our word to ourselves, it becomes harder and harder to keep our word with others. People learn not to count on us because our word is like holding water in a fist: it just trickles out.

It is not only in the conventional world that we can lose our reputation by not keeping our word; this can spill over into our spiritual path as well. So we must rouse our self-confidence and take positive pride in ourselves and our ability to carry out whatever commitments we have made, worldly or spiritual. If it is the bodhisattva path, then it is our commitment to the three wisdoms of hearing, contemplation, and meditation and to diligently train in these as our discipline. Our commitment is not merely to gather the three wisdoms for their own sake, but to apply them in all areas of our confusion and ignorance, wherever our habitual neuroses and disturbing emotions threaten us.

TRANSFORMING NEUROSIS WITH POSITIVE PRIDE

Let's say we are feeling a surge of jealousy. Something has triggered a wave of envious thoughts and jealous emotions. We are self-aware of this. Here, we must first accept what is happening and honestly acknowledge the state of mind and emotions we are experiencing. Then we can become curious. We have the hearing wisdom that knows we can use jealousy as a source of sympathetic joy and rejoice on behalf of others. This knowledge alone is a tremendous advantage. We may still experience the habitual momentum of the jealousy, but we also know that we have options.

Our hearing wisdom gives us the perspective that jealousy is generally a form of aggression, caused by the self feeling threatened. So instead of going down that well-worn path, we rouse our self-confidence and seek out something positive in the object of our jealousy. Instead of thinking, *Why don't I have this? Why does this other person have this?* we can think, *Just as I wish to have this, so must this other person. Just as I have been wanting and working hard to get this thing that they now have, they, too, must have been wanting and working on it. I know that nothing comes without merit, so I can rejoice that they have the merit to receive it now. I can rejoice that their hard work is paying off and imagine that they must feel very glad to have achieved or received this thing.* We can reflect on how they must feel by putting ourselves in their shoes and trying to feel their joy as our own joy.

Contemplating in such ways, led by the hearing wisdom of the Dharma, is precisely how we come to integrate the teachings into our lives. This is what practice is: the obscuration, the wisdom, and our intention to bring these two together all meeting in one place. It is not necessarily easy. Especially in the beginning, it can feel uncomfortable and counterintuitive as the strength of our habit meets the wisdom of the Dharma. But if we stay with and allow these two to mingle, things slowly shift, and we begin to taste liberation—liberation from the tyranny of the self. With the practice of sympathetic joy, for instance, we come to realize that we don't have to have it all for ourselves. In fact, it can be much more joyful to simply rejoice when others' merit and endeavor bring them pleasure, comfort, acclaim, or whatever they wish for. We realize for ourselves what the Buddha meant when he said, "Rejoicing is the purest form of joy."

We must know that we can turn our mind and our emotional states around in a positive direction. By relying on this level of self-confidence in ourself and our ability, we summon the energy of our initial habitual self-centered reaction and turn that into a source of deep and abiding joy. Even though this may initially feel quite foreign and strange, as our mind and heart are not yet conditioned to work in this way, we can still challenge ourselves and learn. Not only can we use the raw material of jealousy and envy, for example, to overcome our negative mindset, but we can also transform it into the positive state of rejoicing. That is the challenge, and that is how we grow. With inspiration and clarity, we joyfully set this challenge for ourselves, and then with time and practice, we work in that direction. However inflexible and tight we may feel in the beginning, the mind is extremely supple and fluid, and it can change. That is why the Buddha said, "If you train your mind it will be your greatest ally and serve as a refuge. If not, it will haunt and imprison you."

We can test ourselves with anything that arises, particularly our painful emotions and mental states. With anger or aggression, we learn to first recognize and acknowledge the habitual self-centered reaction. With interest and curiosity in that moment, we can learn to generate compassion, first for ourself and our own burning state of anger and then for all beings in similar states of mind, knowing that unchecked aggression causes much pain and sorrow in the lives of countless beings. We can then make deep prayers that all the world's aggression and anger be exhausted by our own present experience. If we can't do that in the moment because it is too heated or intense, we can come back to it once we regain our composure. It is never too late to come back and do this. We can return to it weeks or even years after an incident and practice this.

We can similarly recognize and acknowledge the tension that comes with attachment, desire, or greed. We reflect upon the deep anxiety and insecurity that fuels our grasping, which arises from the root of self-cherishing. We can take the personal pain of that state of mind and reach out to connect to those who are also suffering in such states of self-absorption. Generating tender loving kindness, we wish that all beings, including ourselves, be freed from the suffocating experience of self-centered attachments, insecurities, greed, and ultimately from our ignorance, which is the root of all sorrow.

In terms of our ignorance, the confusion of deep mental fog, or *timuk* in Tibetan, we recognize the lack of awareness in our mind and emotions, the sheer state of denial that we are often in. There is much pain in not knowing what is happening or what to do next, what emotions will arise and ravage us, or what unpredictable circumstances might arise, as well as our reactions to those. Confusion, therefore, is not one simple thing that pains us—it is a material that morphs and pervades many areas. Even if we know we are in a state of affliction or a habitual reaction, we often don't know what to do about it. We are like a blind person who has found themselves in the middle of a busy intersection with cars and trucks zooming by. We know we have to get to safety on the other side of the road and are motivated to do so, but we have no idea how to move forward. We sense danger all around.

When we find ourselves feeling the pain of bewilderment, the fear of the unknown, or simply the confusion of not understanding how best to proceed—that is the pain and anguish of deep mental fog.

In this approach, we learn to turn our mind toward using each neurotic mindset or emotion as an opportunity, a starting point to apply our mindfulness and vigilant introspection—bakyö and shézhin—with confidence in ourselves and our ability. We want to remember that this is not a practice of rejection, but rather one of curiosity and growth, of facing our challenges with confidence and courage. Feeling something and rejecting it is different from feeling something and becoming curious and open. It takes mindfulness and some level of *shamatha*, or calm abiding, in order to be present and navigate this difference, which can be subtle.

Whatever happens, we always have the home base of the Dharma to come back to. No matter how lost and distracted we get in our confusions, sidetracks, hopes, and fears, we can always come back. That is why we cultivate the hearing wisdom of the Dharma. Otherwise, when we get lost, we are unsure of what to come back to or how.

53
But if, depressed, I give up trying,
How can I gain freedom from my abject state?
But if I stand my ground with proud resolve,
It will be hard for even great faults to attack me.

54
Therefore, with a steadfast heart
I'll get the better of my weaknesses.
But if my failings get the upper hand,
My wish to overcome the triple world is laughable indeed.

55
"I will be victor over all,
And nothing shall prevail and bring me down!"
The offspring of the Lion, the Conqueror,
Should constantly abide in this self-confidence.

As we discussed, when the five afflicting emotions arise, we want to first recognize what is happening and accept our state of mind. It can be tempting to wallow in self-pity or to justify our thoughts and emotions. If either of those did us any good, perhaps we could consider them, but after countless journeys down those roads, have we ever improved, felt better, or resolved anything? Of course not. It is helpful to see how much we tend to undermine ourselves when we try to justify our stance or wallow in self-pity, rather than simply facing and working directly with what is happening. Complaining, especially internally to ourselves, and habitually focusing on the negative attributes of our lives, our conditions, or what is happening with us—this approach is not bound for success.

We instinctually know this, but how much weight do we give this knowledge, particularly in those moments when we start to spiral downward? It is, of course, up to us. As the Buddha said, "I have shown you the path to liberation, but liberation depends upon you." Others can love and care for us and want us to do well, but if we don't pull ourselves up by our own bootstraps, ultimately no one can do anything for us.

NEVER GIVE UP

In some sense, diligence, or tsöndru, all comes down to not giving up— on the wisdom of the Dharma, on the path, and particularly on ourselves and our potential. All difficulties can be brought onto the path as long as we do not give up on the path and on ourselves. We base our self-confidence on knowing this.

After all, when we generate bodhichitta, we cannot immediately expect to have all the qualities of the enlightened state. As a five-year-old child, we cannot conceive of being a mother or a father. But in time and with age and maturity, many of us become parents. When things seem far away, our human mind has a hard time conceiving of them. In the dead of winter, when we look outside and see the ground covered in snow with not a single green leaf in sight, it is hard to conceive of the lushness and blossoms of early summer. But the flowers and the greenery come. Just because we can't conceive of something or see it presently in front of our eyes doesn't mean that it can't happen.

Everything lies in potential. If there is potential, then in time and with conditions that potential manifests without fail. All sentient beings by nature have the potential to be enlightened. That is what the Mahayana sutras teach. The Buddha taught the emptiness of our perceived dualistic world in the second turning of the Wheel of Dharma, while in the third turning he spoke in depth of Buddha nature or *tathagatagarbha*, referring to our pure essence or potential being fully present, yet obscured. When the obscurations, which are like the clouds that cover the light and warmth of the sun, are purified, then the naturally present potential shines through unobstructed. That is the enlightened state, which is inherently present in all sentient beings.

Getting discouraged and giving up benefit neither oneself nor others. The mindset of giving up leaves no possibility for liberation or freedom; it squeezes all that out. If we are timid with our mind and our neuroses, fearful to face or overcome anything, then our neuroses only grow bigger and bolder. We are like the dying serpent lying on the ground. This is how it is when we give up, lie down, and surrender ourselves to our neuroses and the force of our habitual mind. If we rouse our self-confidence to not give up, especially when we start to feel low, that itself can sustain us and turn things around.

How this can be is not immediately obvious to us, especially in this day and age, with our level of distraction and outward fixation. But in time, with our interest, studies, application of the path, and progress in the stages of development, we will come to see how we, and all beings, can become liberated. This is how our potential thus comes to blossom in full—but only if we don't give up on ourselves.

GENUINE CONFIDENCE
VERSUS ORDINARY PRIDE

56

Those whom arrogance destroys
Are thus defiled; they lack self-confidence.
Those who have true confidence escape the foe,
While others fall into the power of an evil pride.

When working with positive pride or self-confidence, many people wonder: *Isn't this also a neurosis?* No, Shantideva says. This self-confidence is cultivated and nurtured within the context of overcoming our complacency, laziness, and patterns of avoidance. It may look like ordinary pride from the outside, but it is, in fact, a positive state of mind that works against our neurotic, self-centered pride. This positive pride works against attachment, aggression, ignorance, and all the rest of our destructive emotions, or kleshas, which thrive in ignorance and complacency. It gives us a much-needed boost to face our destructive, self-centered habits and neuroses, and eventually helps us attain complete freedom and liberation.

Confidence in our ability to do the work necessary to overcome our destructive states of mind and emotions brings us tremendous ease, wherever we live and wherever we go. We know that we can handle whatever comes our way—whatever conditions arise, whatever threats appear, whatever upheavals may occur. This ultimately comes down to two things: physical and mental resilience. Physically, seeing any pain, illness, or misfortune that may befall us as a purification of our past wrongdoing brings acceptance, which can naturally balance out the experience of pain.

Mentally, the pain of feeling despondent, discouraged, sad, unhappy, or grief-stricken—there is room to experience all of these. At the same time, we see that these are just experiences, as in the story of the old monk who lay dying. When asked how he was doing, he said, "This old monk is suffering quite a bit, but I am doing fine." This may seem like disassociation, but the difference here is that the experience of allowing everything to unfold without holding on to anything as solid and real brings great ease and connection. This is the fruit of studying and practicing tongpa nyi and *dak mépa*, emptiness and egolessness of self.

With interest, aspiration, and confidence, we can work on all of this. Ultimately, nothing sticks to us, but in the meantime, we must work on our *bakchak*, the momentum of old habits that have yet to wear themselves out. The residue or flavor of these takes time to dissolve. As we proceed, however, we become more and more free from our habits and their residue. We know that we can face things and see them through.

Imagine having that kind of confidence, ease, and connection. Imagine knowing that you could genuinely overcome whatever weaknesses or insecurities might arise, whatever dormant conditions might provoke or anger you. Imagine having no doubt that you could face and overcome absolutely anything. It is possible. With consistent application, this kind of practice delivers. It is not a mere hypothesis.

Not long ago, Tibet was invaded. Thousands had to flee for their lives, in many cases with nothing but the clothes on their back. There are innumerable accounts from that time, stories of how people faced this tremendously difficult and painful time with extraordinary courage and confidence. In Amdo, in northeastern Tibet, the invading armies rounded up the heads of the monasteries along with local lords and leaders. After lining them up, the invaders began to execute them one by one. When they came to the head lama of one monastery, the lama asked his executioner to wait a moment so that he could say a short prayer. The army commander on the scene allowed this. With his hands in prayer the lama said, "May I, with all my own negativities, take upon myself the negativity of all living beings, and may this purify the wrongdoing of myself and others. For this person who is about to kill me, may I take the karma of his crime upon myself and purify all his negativity." The lama opened his eyes and said, "OK, I am ready," and they shot him. Someone who witnessed this later recounted the incident to His Holiness the Dalai Lama. His Holiness often quotes this story to illustrate the benefit and power of training one's mind thoroughly in the bodhichitta practice.

We all must die. We all must face hardships, loss, and possibly many other unknown tragedies, along with all the joys, pleasures, and ups and downs of life. The gift of bodhichitta—of training in tenderness and altruism with joyful diligence and commitment—truly transforms the mind. As this story of the head lama illustrates, such practices can blossom into extraordinary courage and ease, even moments before one's own execution.

57

When arrogance inflates the mind,
It draws it down to states of misery—
Or ruins happiness, should human birth be gained.
Thus one is born a slave, dependent for one's sustenance,

58

Or feebleminded, ugly, without strength,
The butt and laughingstock of everyone.
These "ascetics" puffed up with conceit!
If these you call the proud, then tell me who are wretched?

59

Those who uphold pride to vanquish pride, the enemy,
Are truly proud, victorious, and brave.
And they who stem the increase of that evil pride,
Perfect, according to their wish, the fruit of victory for beings.

These verses continue to drive home the critical distinction between ordinary pride or arrogance and positive pride. One important difference is that the neurosis of ego-based pride is always used against others. Because such pride is based on the ego, it brings with it attachment to the self and aggression toward others. Positive pride, on the other hand, is used to overcome our own internal neurosis, which brings us down. There is no aggression toward others and no ego-based puffing up of the self. The puffed-up high of ego-based pride is shaky and disconnected from others, while positive pride is grounded—humble even—and integrated with those around us and all sentient beings.

Furthermore, genuine self-confidence or positive pride never loses appreciation for others who have attributes similar to our own or qualities equal to what we value or even better than we can imagine possessing. Positive pride and genuine self-confidence always have room to appreciate others with a clean heart and mind. With ego-based pride, others' attributes and qualities usually feel like a threat. The conceit of the self leaves us no room to appreciate others.

People who overcome or consciously work with their ego-based limitations and hindrances are admirable. They possess palpable strength and confidence. Those who have healthy self-confidence inspire others, especially as they face and overcome hardships, like the blind person who climbed Mt. Everest. Such people and instances are awe-inspiring. Why? Because we all recognize the strength and goodness of grounded self-confidence in the face of great hardship. That kind of strength is powerful and attractive. When we come under the influence of or lose ourselves to neurosis, we become weaker and feebler, not strong and respectable.

The human psyche is incredibly intelligent. For the most part, we know when someone has genuine self-confidence and positive pride versus someone who is merely arrogant and puffed up. Genuine self-confidence brings benefit both to oneself and to others. External provocations, threats, or even executioners can't easily bring down a person with authentic self-confidence. The confidence that overcomes neuroses is, therefore, nothing but positive. But ordinary pride that arrogantly holds oneself to be better than or above others—make no mistake, that kind of pride will destroy us.

Verses 60–62 discuss cultivating the third kind of self-confidence or pride with regard to overcoming our afflictive emotions.

60
When I am beleaguered by defilements,
I will stand and face them in a thousand ways.
I'll not surrender to the host of the afflictions
But like a lion I will stand amid a crowd of foxes.

Confidence is not something floating around out there that we have to capture. It comes from inside of us: not by adding things on, but by letting go—letting go of the self. We often want things to happen in certain ways according to our own preferences, but we are not necessarily willing to let go of anything from our own side. We want the return without making the investment. We want friendships and want people to be attracted to us, but we don't want to be generous. We want to put out the fire, but we don't want to use our own water because we are attached to keeping that water for ourselves. Action and intention, therefore, do not meet. We don't want to stretch, extend, or let go. This timidity or shrinking away prevents us from accomplishing our aspirations. The good news is that confidence is not built by accumulating or holding on to things; it is built by letting go. While it is not initially easy, letting go is much easier than accumulating or holding on.

There are always growing pains. If we reject the necessary pain or discomfort of growth, we will never progress. We need to develop some healthy tolerance to the pain of growth. We can do this by generating a joyful outlook toward learning what it takes to make our actions meet our intentions. Much of this comes down to letting go of the self and its tenacious preferences.

We may have the wish to benefit others, but if we can't overcome—or at least learn to work with—our self-clinging, neuroses, laziness, complacency, and habitual patterns, then isn't it a bit of a bluff to think about benefiting others? Stabilizing our mind in self-confidence, particularly regarding our potential, is critical for overcoming laziness and lack of inspiration. Working on this becomes our own personal victory, and the benefit of others is also assured. So we must never give up, but rather rouse our self-confidence and tell ourselves that we can do this. Even if we fall down, forget, or mess up a million times, if we remain determined to never give up, we will reach our goal, especially if the goal is the altruistic path of the bodhisattva. We will get there joyfully, one step at a time, one challenge at a time.

THE POWER OF RESOLVE

61
However great may be their peril,
People will by reflex guard their eyes.
And likewise I, whatever dangers come,
Must not fall down beneath defilement's power.

62

Better for me to be burned to death,
And better to be killed, my head cut off!
At no time will I bow and scrape
Before that foe of mine, defiled emotion.

62a

Thus in every time and place
I will not wander from the wholesome path.

If we find ourselves in a dangerous situation, our first thought naturally goes to the safety of our body, and we instinctively first protect
our eyes. Similarly, whatever challenges we face in our life or our spiritual path, we must always work to protect our bodhichitta. It is not
that we won't, as I mentioned, fall down, forget, or mess up—in fact,
it is not really about that at all. It is about our resolve. We do not want
to waste our energy on trying to be perfect and then become devas-
tated when we don't measure up to our own self-imposed pressure or
inflated standard. That is a diversion. Instead, we must learn to guard
our resolve and protect our bodhichitta, just as we would reflexively
guard our eyes.

Paraphrasing Mahatma Gandhi's famous quote, "They can beat me,
and they can break my bones, but they cannot take away my self-respect."*
We want to rouse the spirit that says, *Anyone can do anything they want
from the outside, but no one can make me surrender to my neurosis or lose
my own bodhichitta.* Or, similarly, *I might mess up, I might not get it right, I
might succumb to my habitual patterns and self-centeredness, but I won't let
that be the end of the story. I will come back to my bodhichitta practice. That
will be my home base, my ultimate reference point. I might get angry or get
lost in excitement, but I resolve to reflect on this and ultimately come back
to the four immeasurables, and to equalizing and exchanging self and other.*
Like the head lama in Amdo, we should think, *Even if someone comes to*

---

* Diana L. Eck, "Gandhi in Egypt," *Harvard Crimson*, March 2, 2011, https://www.the
-crimson.com/article/2011/3/2/nonviolent-sharp-gandhi-people/.

cut off my head, I won't just surrender to my neurosis or my anger, which is by far my greatest enemy.

In a similar vein, the Buddha said that the Dharma will never be destroyed by an outer force. A lion cannot be destroyed or overcome by any outer foes in the jungle, but they can be eaten slowly from within by tiny worms. The Buddhadharma, too, can only be destroyed from within—meaning by giving in to our neuroses, our self-importance, and our ego-based drives.

Our hearing wisdom has taught us that all our disturbing neurotic emotions come from believing in and clinging to a self. We know intellectually that no self exists in the way in which we cling to it, but based on the momentum of our habitual reactions, the urge to cherish the self with attachment and to protect the self with aggression automatically arises. As a further expression of those tendencies, pride develops as an extension of our attachment, and jealousy arises as an extension of our aggression. Knowing this much from our hearing wisdom allows us to apply mindfulness and vigilant introspection—bakyö and shézhin— and especially to be curious about objectively contemplating our mind and emotions.

What we are seeking is the ability to expand our intelligence and our compassion by reflecting upon and then reducing our level of self-importance and self-attachment. There are many teachings that we can contemplate to reduce self-attachment and better understand our ignorance. The four immeasurables practice, in particular, greatly balances out the primal force of our attachment to the self. It is important to understand that attachment to the self does not go away completely, and this is not necessarily the goal we seek. We seek to reduce our attachment to the self to a manageable level. We keep a healthy dose of self-love or care, but meanwhile, we work on our extra-strength self-importance and our mindless, habitual reactivity. As we apply ourselves to the four immeasurables and exchanging self and other, our self-centeredness becomes much more manageable. That awareness and manageability, more than complete eradication, are our goal.

Personally working with our mind and emotions helps us take the teachings and our own application and confidence to heart, more than just as a hobby. Applying ourselves when we become tight and fixated, when our heart closes, or when we become irritated, impatient, and judgmental—these are precisely the times to work with the Dharma, and this is what transforms us. Working through our own challenges and painful mindsets and emotions helps us to open tenderly to others who are in the very same predicament. It is not a mystery of hit or miss. It is all completely doable, and it is within our reach.

The fear and anxiety that most of us suffer from are focused almost completely outward, as if something external is happening or is going to happen to us. If there is no true "reactor," meaning if we have even a rough understanding of dak mépa, egolessness of self, then we can ask ourselves, *Who is there to be truly fearful? Who is there to react? Where is that self, the reactor?* It may seem like things are threatening us from the outside, and there might be something that needs to be addressed outwardly, but our anxious emotion essentially comes down to the fear of our own mind. The root of our fear is fear of our mind's reactiveness— as if it were out of our control. As we apply the four immeasurables both on and off the cushion, we become softer and more spacious. And as we realize the empty and luminous nature of our mind, we further see that there is no need for such fear. It's not that the experience is not there: it can arise as an experience, but the experience is less heavy, more transparent.

This is how we begin to understand the notion of *rochik*, or one taste. If we are more seated in the way things are and not as caught up in the way things appear or in our reactions to those appearances, we thus allow the nature of all things to shine through their appearances. When we speak of rochik, it doesn't mean that everything is bland and all the same. All appearances still have their own distinctive natural vitality and energy. But we also remain cognizant of their empty-luminous nature, their inability to be pinpointed as "real." This allows us to enjoy the variety of appearances without being sucked in or thrown off, no matter how things might manifest. The discovery, realization, and especially the stabilization of our nature of mind develop from time spent on our cushion, from personally familiarizing ourselves with that nature—the nature of all phenomena—and experiencing how that nature pervades all appearances both inwardly and outwardly.

Nightmares only threaten us when we are asleep. As soon as we wake up from all that was occurring in our dream state, we wonder, *What happened to it; where did it go?* When we wake up to our own nature of mind, what once seemed like a nightmare experience of negative emotions, upheavals, and confusion no longer threatens us. If we remain sleeping, but know how to have a lucid dream and are aware of our dream while dreaming, then even the appearance of a nightmare does not have the same hold over us. What was terrifying in a nightmare can be humorous or fascinating in a lucid dream. We no longer feel threatened or fearful.

For someone with a stable nature of mind practice, everything they experience is interesting, fresh, and enjoyable. Continually establishing ourselves in the nature or simply having faith in the emptiness teachings allows us to relate to everything that arises as one taste but with infinite freshness in the variety of experiences. This is achieved through diligence: joyfully putting our butt on our cushion and putting the teachings into practice internally, rather than mindlessly wasting time with all the distractions that can eat up our day.

In our practice of diligence and joyfully facing our subtle levels of laziness, we want to remember that, just as all the sages of the past accomplished the path, we can do so as well. We have exactly the same potential; we have a connection to the same teachings they studied and practiced, and we have the same twenty-four hours in a day that they had. Our job now is to have confidence and remind ourselves not to be forgetful and lazy—to have resolve.

This concludes the second ally, that of cultivating steadfastness through three kinds of self-confidence.

21

A MEANINGFUL LIFE

In verses 63–66, Shantideva covers the third ally of joy.

63
Like those who take great pleasure in their games,
Whatever task the Bodhisattvas do,
Let them devote themselves without reserve,
With joyfulness that never knows satiety.

We should do what we want to do. If we discover something that truly supports our mind now and in the future, then we must take deep delight in embracing and practicing that. When we are sane and grounded, with a well-rounded perspective on what is most meaningful and beneficial in life, then engaging in the practice of Dharma is the greatest joy. Many great masters, such as my root teacher Dilgo Khyentse Rinpoche, exemplify this. He took great joy in his life and was playful, carefree, and completely at ease even when things were challenging. He was a great realized being, and he deeply enjoyed all aspects of life. We can take such beings as examples and remind ourselves of what it means to enjoy life even when things are problematic.

Most of us don't think much about our internal life and how to secure that, now or in the future. Just as today came, tomorrow will also come. Just as we do things to secure our conventional lives like shopping for food for the week or filling our car with enough gas to make a journey, we also want to inwardly prepare ourselves for the future. This does not contradict our enjoyment of the present moment; in fact, it makes the present moment more meaningful and enjoyable. We can enjoy the present more fully when we know that our present circumstances are also securing our future. It is like the farmer who sows seeds well for a future harvest. They expect an abundant crop while planting and are not disturbed that they can't pick the fruit or reap the harvest as they are sowing seeds. We are presently a product of our past actions and intentions, and our current actions and intentions will likewise bear fruit in future circumstances. In securing our future, we reestablish and reinvest our current capital for a better and better outcome.

We thus want to learn to wake up looking forward to beginning our day with practice, like children who get up and can't wait to go outside and play with their friends. Play is always on a child's mind. Children go to sleep thinking about playing and wake up looking forward to playing. Children never get enough of playing. They find so much joy engaging in play. It is not so much about the specific activity, but the energy and the mindset of play that so captivate them. We want to be like this when it comes to our practice of the paramitas in our life.

As we get the taste of practice, we also get the taste of the deep joy that practice brings. The joy of our activities for the benefit of others then radiates from our heart and mind. This is true even if we are doing something small or seemingly mundane, like helping our neighbor carry boxes, picking our kids up from school, making a meal for our family, or filling our offering bowls and sitting down to meditate.

Just as an elephant plunges into a cool lake in summer with relief and delight, as we get the hang of Dharma practice and what it does for our life and mind, we dive into our practice mind with similar joy and relief—particularly our formal meditation practice. It feels so good to sit down and rest our mind and to generate loving kindness and compassion for all beings. It feels nourishing and delightful to wholesomely relate to our rising thoughts and emotions and to equalize and exchange ourselves with others. We come to feel that we can never get enough joy from our practice, especially our bodhichitta practice. Practice becomes like this—food for our soul, balm for our heart, and medicine for our painfully inflamed states of mind. We realize that there is so much joy in this, and we can simply be joyful in our practice. All of this begins with a decision and a conscious intention and interest to move in this direction.

64

People labor hard to gain contentment
Though success is very far from sure.
But how can they be happy if they do not do
Those deeds that are the source of joy to them?

In the conventional world, people work so hard for just a little glimpse of so-called happiness, trying to build a life, make a home together, create a family, and so on. It's not that these things can't bring us happiness; they can, to a certain degree and for a short while. At the same time, we also know that often things don't work out. Much of the time this kind of conventional happiness remains just out of reach, even if we seemingly have all the elements in place. This can be tremendously confusing, especially for young people. We grow up seeing depictions of how life "should" be in ads or movies, on social media, and through the general cultural influences in our lives. In this world of illusion, we love to sell each other illusions. Unfortunately, most of us take the bait, and we try so hard, consciously and unconsciously, to measure up to often unrealistic images of "normal life."

We often see, where there is a chance of securing happiness, that something suddenly comes in and destroys the happy situation. A couple builds a house, for instance, and just as it is about to be finished, they start to argue and bicker, and a small issue blows up into a huge situation. Instead of moving in, they end up getting divorced and selling the house they worked to build together. All their plans and hopes of that being a place to start a family and bring them happiness go out the door. When there is almost a chance of happiness, something comes in, seemingly out of the blue, and destroys it. I have observed this time and again, in others and in myself. We are just about to get to a place that we have been aiming for, and then something happens and dashes the plan.

It is not anyone's fault. This is just the nature of samsara, the nature of grasping at ephemeral projections and images of so-called happiness, which generally disappoint us in the end. Samsara is based on trying to hold something together that, by nature, is bound to fall apart. All compounded things are impermanent and subject to change. There is nothing wrong with this; it is just the way things are. Samsara is perpetuated when, instead of accepting this and turning inward to work with our mind, we wish things weren't the way they are and try to do everything we can to change or rearrange them. Wishing things were different from how they are is the crux of our suffering in samsara.

65

And since they never have enough of pleasure,
Honey on the razor's edge,
How could they have enough of merit,
Fruits of which are happiness and peace?

Conventional happiness, or the happiness found in samsara—the happiness we seek from grasping and trying to capture what is by nature always changing—is like licking honey off a razor blade. The initial taste is sweet, but there is pain in the end. We easily start various pursuits, all aimed at success and happiness, but how many of these work out or are fulfilled? How many of these don't end up in disappointment or a painful place? It is like a spending spree—buying things on our credit card is easy, but when the bill comes at the end of the month, it can be a big headache and heartache.

On the other hand, more meaningful pursuits like the Dharma can be harder to initiate and take hold of. But once we develop a habit with something like the practice of the six paramitas or the four immeasurables and the practice of virtue, not only do such things get easier as we apply ourselves and progress, but our joy increases with each engagement. Dilgo Khyentse Rinpoche often used to quote a famous saying: "Conventional pursuits are easy in the beginning, but get harder and harder as you proceed. Dharma is harder in the beginning, but gets easier and easier as you progress."

Often, when we are having a hard time or things are not going as we planned or wished, we hold outer parties or circumstances responsible. Maybe outer conditions and circumstances do disappoint us at times. But we generally blame external factors 100 percent and then work to change or rearrange a million outer conditions, thinking that will fix things, make us feel better, or empower us. It might make us feel better for a short while, mainly due to the preoccupying distraction of changing our situation. But if we have not worked with our mind, our challenges and difficulties tend to follow us around no matter where we go or what we try to change on the outside. This is a lesson that life eventually teaches us.

When our mind is split, when we are not willing to face what we are experiencing, this makes challenges truly challenging. Our biggest pain is when a conflict of interest seizes our mind and heart and we internally wish that things were different from how they are. If our mind is not split, if we are able to accept whatever is arising for us karmically and then work from there to expand our heart, learn new things, adjust our perspective, or look at things from various angles, then we find that we can enjoy even the most challenging of circumstances. Perhaps this is not like enjoying a cocktail party, but we can take pleasure in the process and the presence of mind that enable us to navigate with compassion and tenderness.

We might be reading this wondering, *How do I get from feeling pressured to practice as another thing to check off my to-do list to feeling joy and ease and actually looking forward to being on my meditation cushion with my mind?* We know that we have a connection to Dharma, bodhichitta practice, and the four immeasurables, and we long for meaning in our lives—but formal practice has somehow become a chore.

One way to work with this is to actively walk ourselves through various scenarios. Let's say we are doing a meditation session. We have sat down to do a half hour of meditation on the four immeasurables or shamatha practice. We are sitting there fine for a few minutes, starting to gather our mind and energy, and then all of a sudden we remember that we forgot to reply to a text message from someone. Our mind and body become restless, and we want to reach for our phone. Before reaching out or jumping up, give yourself a minute. Take that minute and stop trying to meditate or do any formal practice. Instead, openly ask, *What do I want to do exactly? If I get up and write this text right now, what will that accomplish? What will that experience feel like precisely? Will I be truly satisfied if I accomplish this thing I want to do right now? And does it have to be done right now, in this half hour of time that I have set aside for myself to relate to my mind and life in a meaningful way?*

Instead of mindlessly zooming off with our restless energy, which we know will make us feel uneasy later, undermining our self-confidence especially regarding what nourishes us the most, why not take a few minutes and let ourselves explore the answers to the above questions?

Think it through. Imagine doing whatever it is that you think you want to do and what it will bring you. Visualize it clearly, and go through the motions step-by-step, from beginning to end. Thinking things through in this detailed way can bring us back, inspire us, and reconnect us to our practice and ourselves.

Once we feel a bit of space or relief from the urgency to jump up and go, we can then reflect on what we accomplish through our practice. When we are able to practice, do our mind and body come to be at ease? Do we come to feel light and agile, and does experience become more luminous? Do we have glimpses of seeing our thoughts for what they are: transparent and fleeting? Reflect on the deeper joy and well-being that we feel after completing a good session of the four immeasurables or shamatha meditation. Thinking things through in this way grounds our mind, drawing on our inner resources and creativity to reestablish our connection to our own deeper state of being. A session of practice spent in such reflection can be much more meaningful, productive, and satisfying than just sitting there, staring out into space and waiting for the time to be up.

We all long to be grounded and connected to ourselves, not just running on fumes or lulled into inertia by the relentless waves of distracting preoccupations. This method of thinking things through with scenarios can be helpful whenever we feel scattered, distracted, or dull. This is how we can complete our session with ease and joy—a joy that increases as we proceed in this way.

Another thing to remember is that our distracted, scattered energy will change and shift no matter what. But if we give up on our goals too easily, yielding to that distracted energy and its momentum, the habit of giving up becomes more and more entrenched. Rather than using the opportunity of whatever arises to strengthen our practice mind, we instead become a slave to our distractions. This habit not only hurts our spiritual path, it can also spread into other areas of our life. Eventually, we can find it hard to keep our focus and see anything through.

This approach of the Diligence Chapter, relying on the four allies and two strengths, supports and encourages us to see our commitments through. When we encounter challenges to accomplishing our aspirations or goals, often we either throw up our hands or else bear down and grit our teeth in order to get through it. Neither approach is sustainable, nor is either very enjoyable. If we can honestly reflect and process what is arising for us, that is often enough to clear the air and ease our tension, allowing us to freely proceed. It is also a wonderful way to spend time with oneself.

So many of us are afraid of being alone, especially with our own mind. If we can be present with ourselves on our cushion and engage the three wisdoms of hearing, contemplation, and meditation, that time alone can be tremendously meaningful and enjoyable. We can continue that joy in the post-meditation with the six paramitas and learn to meet whatever arises with cheerfulness, even when it is challenging or painful.

66

The elephant, tormented by the noonday sun,
Will dive into the waters of a lake,
And likewise I must plunge into my work
That I might bring it to completion.

Like an elephant who, in the midst of the summer heat, blissfully plunges into the cooling waters of a lake, we want to dive into our practice or whatever task we have at hand. We want to learn to enjoy whatever we must do, giving ourselves wholeheartedly to our task or activity, like an elephant thoroughly enjoying a bath in a lake. Or we could think of a Labrador retriever swimming in the local reservoir on a hot summer day or a swan alighting on a body of water—each of these examples gives us an image of the pleasure we can feel upon diving wholeheartedly into our work or our practice.

22

TAKING BREAKS

In verse 67, Shantideva covers the fourth ally of taking breaks.

67

If impaired by weakness or fatigue,
I'll lay the work aside, the better to resume.
And I will leave the task when it's complete,
All avid for the work that's next to come.

Taking breaks is an important part of diligence practice. We want to be mindful of how we are proceeding with any given pursuit. If we notice we are becoming overzealous, too attached to our experiences, or pushing harder than what seems natural, those are usually signs that we should ease off and take a short break. Sometimes it feels good to practice, and we want to keep going and going and going, making the session longer and longer. We can burn ourselves out this way by becoming attached to a certain aspect of meditation practice. After the initial high of our experience wears off or if we can't find that feeling again, we might be confused, let down, or uninspired. Rather than practicing for seven hours straight and then not doing it again for another year, we can instead try meditating for shorter periods on a regular basis and slowly building upon that.

All of us can become attached to experiences or sensations or states of mind—it happens. We get into a groove and it captures us, and we keep going until we literally can't do it anymore—like working into the wee hours of the morning, binge-watching a TV series, exercising until we feel we might collapse, or doing anything to extremes. This is how we burn out. We can't maintain any level of activity that is driven by a lot of clinging and attachment or that doesn't include some downtime. It is not possible to maintain any kind of extreme on a consistent basis.

With practice, we initially tend to set high goals that are impossible to achieve. That is natural in the beginning, but eventually we want to learn to set a manageable, reasonable amount of time to practice and just do that much. Then we take a break and come back and do another session in the same way as consistently as possible. This is how we make progress: step by step, sustainably, reasonably. We start small and build slowly.

This may not be inspiring for some of us. We feel the excitement and inspiration to achieve great things—to renounce the world, be a yogin, live in a cave like Milarepa . . . now that is something we can get excited and inspired about. Of course, this is wonderful to aspire to, but if we wish to be like Milarepa, we also have to be inspired to do our meditation practice in our room or wherever we are every day, whether we feel excited about it or not.

Practice is meant to progress stage by stage. Dreaming too grandly, even on the spiritual path, can be a pitfall. This instruction on taking breaks is meant to temper our habit of grasping at big ideas and help us attain a sustainable level of effort. Otherwise, if our ambition or our drive gets the better of us and we keep pushing, we can wear ourselves out. Taking a break and resting our mind and body allow us to come back refreshed and ready to reengage. When we are standing at the bottom of a mountain, we don't expect to jump right up to the top. We get to the summit by walking steadily and consistently, putting one foot in front of the other, taking breaks to rest and recover, and then resuming our upward progress.

This is how we accomplish anything; it is how the antidote works on the neurosis and how realization works on the obscuration. One moment of a candle's flame does not eliminate the darkness for more than that moment. Darkness is dispelled by one moment after another sequentially, a continuous succession of moments of a wick burning bright. On the path of liberation, it is not one big *boom* of realization and then that's it—we are enlightened. It is a gradual, sequential, continual process that builds with time and effort. We thus want to take care not to become too driven or ambitious to achieve instantaneous realization or a big *boom*. This is a process of ripening and maturing, and thus consistency is key.

So, should we become fatigued while engaged in our practice or other meaningful activities, we want to pause and mindfully leave it for a bit so that we can take a rest and then resume. If we come down with a cold or the flu, we must also take a break in order to heal ourselves. And in times of pilgrimage or other major events, if we need to leave our daily practice for a few days to engage with what is happening, we do so, and take joy in that particular occasion. Then, once again with great joy, we come back and resume our regular schedule.

Up until this point, we have been covering the first and second aspects of the Diligence Chapter: "Do not be downcast," or jéluk mépa in Tibetan, which means learning to be free of laziness, and "Marshal all your powers," or pungtsok in Tibetan, which refers to gathering the four allies. We have covered möpa or aspiration, tenpa or steadfastness, gawa or joy, and now dorwa, or taking breaks, the last of the four allies.

23

THE TWO STRENGTHS

We now move into the third and fourth aspects of the Diligence Chapter: "Make an effort" and "Be the master of yourself." These are the two strengths, lhur langwa and wangdu jawa. As we will recall, lhur langwa, or making an effort, in essence means to practice, practice, practice, without succumbing to distractions. As soon as we notice distractions arising and pulling us away from what we are doing, we must pause. We pause so that we can understand what is happening internally. Here the specific instruction is to apply mindfulness and vigilant introspection, bakyö and shézhin. Our mind naturally possesses these two aspects or qualities, but we call upon them more pointedly when we feel the pull of a distraction or a habit so that we may become more aware and familiar with the undercurrents of our mind.

MAKE AN EFFORT

Verses 68–74 cover the first strength, lhur langwa, or "make an effort."

68
As seasoned fighters face the swords
Of enemies upon the battle line,
I'll lightly dodge the weapons of defilement,
And strike my enemy upon the quick.

69

If, in the fray, the soldier drops his sword,
In fright, he swiftly takes it up again.
So likewise, if the arm of mindfulness is lost,
In fear of hell, I'll quickly get it back!

Shakyamuni Buddha was born as a prince into the Kshatriya, or warrior caste, of India and therefore learned a great deal about warfare and
strategy when he was young. From birth he was destined to become
the king of the Shakyas, until he renounced his throne and sought to
find the truth. Shantideva, along with many others, was from the same
warrior caste. Having trained in these skills from early ages, they could
easily relate to examples of warfare and strategy.

In Buddhism, the battle is not external. It is with our own kleshas,
negative habits, and ego. These are our most sinister enemies. If we
let them run wild, they will endlessly torment and ultimately destroy
us. In the Patience Chapter of *The Way of the Bodhisattva*, Shantideva
says, "If you cannot conquer your own aggression, killing outer oppo-
nents is utterly pointless." Here, in the Diligence Chapter, Shantideva
gives us instructions on how to embrace mindfulness, or bakyö. While
fighting on a battlefield, we never want to drop our sword or weapon
as we know that we would be killed. It is the same with mindfulness.
If we drop our mindfulness, we know that we will be hit hard with
our neuroses and our reactive mind. Mindfulness protects us. It is
something that we keep coming back to and that serves as a guard. It
is like remembering to keep two hands on the wheel and both eyes on
the road while driving.

As practitioners, we always apply mindfulness to our own mind—
we are mindful of what arises, particularly regarding our afflicting, destructive emotions and negative habits. Before these have a chance to
take hold, gain momentum, and destroy us, we want to act preemptively
so that our wisdom mind can maintain the upper hand, keep our "edge,"
and prevent these habits from gaining strength and control.

In addition to mindfulness, we employ the mind's natural capacity
for shézhin, vigilant introspection. Shézhin is an aspect of our mind's

natural intelligence that knows, in this case, why we must overcome our habitual reactions. Shézhin understands how our habitual reactions have harmed us in the past and present and how they will continue to harm us in the future if left unchecked. Perhaps the most important feature of shézhin is that it can discern when these reactions are happening and how the neuroses manifest in our mind. Using our own intelligence—in this case the aspect of introspection—to develop deeper clarity makes us brave and confident to face whatever may arise without feeling intimidated by outer or inner circumstances.

Should we meet with success and achieve our aspirations and wishes, our shézhin knows how to keep us grounded—not lost in the clouds, puffed up, or disconnected from our surroundings. If we face great loss or misfortune, shézhin also keeps us balanced so we do not become utterly destroyed by circumstances. Shézhin supports us so we don't lose ourselves, even regarding how we physically hold ourselves in our body, along with how we relate to our neuroses or various circumstances.

It is important to remember that we don't apply our mindfulness and vigilant introspection in an adverse or aggressive manner toward our destructive emotions, habitual patterns, or painful states of mind. We use our discriminative intelligence to objectively understand and assess the overall situation. From this perspective, we recall the reason for applying the remedy and how our positive states of mind support us—not with attachment to those positive states, but with the clarity of perspective and discriminative intelligence. We take time to analyze how we are served by letting go of our self-centered habitual emotional reactions and by adopting altruism and a tender open heart toward all beings—including ourselves. This brings us peace, and ultimately leads to liberation. Vigilant introspection, or shézhin, is thus a beautiful marriage between our experience and our intelligence.

70
Just as poison fills the body,
Borne on the current of the blood,
Likewise evil, when it finds its chance,
Will spread and permeate the mind.

If we are nicked, even slightly, with a poisoned spear tip, that poison will circulate through our blood and eventually kill us. When we lose our mindfulness, even slightly, many things can happen without our realizing it. Someone might be gossiping, for instance, and we are so intrigued by the juiciness of what we are hearing that, before we know it, we are drawn in and join the conversation. This is precisely where we must be most mindful—wherever we are most lured. Once we join the gossip, it is hard to extract ourselves. Thus, the first pointer when taking up the strength of lhur langwa is to be mindful and vigilantly introspective.

71
I will be like a frightened man, a brimming oil-jar in his hand,
And menaced by a swordsman saying,
"Spill one drop and you shall die!"
This is how practitioners should hold themselves.

If we could realize that we are in a life-and-death situation, we would be extremely careful. This doesn't necessarily mean being tense, but certainly highly aware. Similarly, with driving, we know that we must be careful and exercise awareness whenever we get behind the wheel. We know a car can be a lethal weapon, so we take care, look in all directions, and are mindful when we navigate in traffic. At the same time, we are also relaxed. As the great Tibetan yogini Machik Labdron famously instructed, "Be relaxed yet vigilant, and vigilant yet relaxed." Driving a car is a great example of how to be relaxed yet vigilant and mindful. This verse is pointing to a level of mindfulness that we already have, but often don't realize or capitalize on.

72
Just as a man would swiftly stand
If in his lap a serpent were to glide,
If sleep and lethargy beset me,
I will speedily repulse them.

Here again, Shantideva is giving us a vivid image to remember. Images can be very helpful because in a flash they can communicate so much. In this case the image has to do with how we should respond to the neurosis of laziness or lethargy, of wanting to sleep or avoid things. If a snake slithered onto our lap, would we sit there and let it move freely? Probably not. We would leap up and shake it off. Likewise, if our hair caught fire, we wouldn't simply let it burn; we would run to a faucet or grab a towel and put it out.

When even small neuroses arise or are provoked, we don't want to pretend like nothing is happening and let them go down their usual track or brain pathway. We want to respond mindfully, with vigilance. If there is a subtle feeling of resentment festering inside of us, for instance, we want to address our mind and relate to the internal source of that resentment with reflection, loving kindness, equanimity, and compassion.

73
Every time, then, that I fail,
I will reprove and chide myself,
Thinking long that, by whatever means,
Such faults in future shall no more occur.

Whenever neurosis hits us, if we cannot avoid it overcoming us in the heat of the moment, we must commit to analyzing what happened after the fact. We should not underestimate the value of such retrospection— not to scold or be hard on ourselves, but to understand clearly what triggered us. When we have calmed down and have some quiet time a day or so later, we can return to the incident and reflect: *Why and how did this arise, what triggered it, and how did it all unfold? Where did I fall short or become blinded?*

We can reflect on what provoked us and when our response changed from conscious to habitual. When did we lose our awareness of our universal self and shut down into self-protection or self-cherishing? We rouse our mindfulness and vigilant introspection to focus on how to change our responses for the better, especially the next time around. We accomplish this by fully analyzing what happened and why, not blaming anything outside, but objectively assessing what aspects of our self-cherishing and self-protecting mechanisms were triggered. This is how we can avoid repeating our neurosis over and over again in the future; this is how we can change our habits for the better.

INTEREST AND EDUCATION

Another important point to analyze and continually clarify is our interest. What are we truly interested in? If it is the path of liberation and altruism, then we are naturally inspired to learn more and proceed in that direction. We are inspired to apply our learning, gain insight and experience, and develop faith. Our level of interest determines our level of faith in what we are doing, as well as our level of joy and diligence to go deeper and deeper. If we come at this, not as an intellectual exercise or as a feel-good pursuit, but with genuine interest to take it as far as we can in this life and with the vision to continue into our next life and beyond, we will undoubtedly make progress in that direction.

If you are reading this, you are most probably highly educated, holding a degree or working as an administrator, manager, doctor, lawyer, scientist, writer, artist, health-care giver, educator, engineer, computer programmer, and so on. Our modern education system is amazing, offering us tremendous advantages in the conventional world. The education system of Dharma, however, is different.

Since the 1800s, as the education system in the West developed, the focus was teaching people how to perform necessary tasks in particular fields of work or study. Generally speaking, there was, and is, very little emphasis or training on how to think deeply or to objectively analyze things—outwardly or inwardly. In particular, there is no education on how to work with or understand our mind and emotions and how they function and interact. We are mainly taught how to *do* things—great, useful things, yes—but not how to analyze or understand the functions of the mind objectively or on a personal level.

However great our progress in science and technology has been—

and we undeniably benefit from that progress and must be a part of it—it is still only one kind of education. It does not touch the inner world of our mind. Though we are outwardly focused much of the time, we, in fact, live in the inner world of our mind—and we experience the suffering of not understanding how to relate well to our mind. Much of that internal confusion and suffering can't be helped or changed by science and technology. So, in addition to the education that our Western system has developed, it is also important to learn how to relate to our thought processes, our emotions, our confusions and conflicts, and our joys and sorrows. Rather than simply being subject to our mind's reactiveness and all its associated ups and downs, we want to understand how the mind works and functions so that we can be in the driver's seat.

In Buddhism, through mindfulness and self-reflection, we learn to understand and work through our habits with awareness. We learn to understand and intelligently relate to our mind's emotions. If, on top of our Western education, we can also pursue the inner education system of the Buddhadharma, then our education will be much more comprehensive and well-rounded. From this perspective, we want to value our study and practice of the Dharma, especially in the area of how to reason, assess our experiences, and apply the skillful means of the Buddha's wisdom, especially those found in the contemplations on the four immeasurables. In this way we become genuinely one with the Dharma. This is how we integrate the Dharma into our lives.

74
At all times and in any situation,
How can I make mindfulness my constant habit?
Thinking thus I will desire
To meet with teachers and fulfill the proper tasks.

Mindfulness, or bakyö, is simply being aware of one's inner experience, while vigilant introspection, or shézhin, is our critical intelligence that determines what is and is not helpful and supportive to us. Bakyö is the kind of alertness and carefulness we would maintain while walking beside a steep cliff. Shézhin knows what means to apply and how to use those means to accomplish what we set out to do. Bakyö and shézhin are indispensable strengths of mind. They serve as a ground on which to maintain a joyful attitude, grow our intelligent discernment, and inspire ourselves with confidence. When we study, applying the three wisdoms of hearing, contemplating, and meditating, these methods and mindsets naturally grow more and more familiar, eventually becoming second nature to us. These are the strengths of diligence, or tsöndru. They are strengths of our own mind—not something we acquire from the outside.

Overcoming obstacles by reflecting on impermanence and death, practicing self-inspiration through reasoning, and applying the four allies through consistent mindfulness and vigilant introspection—all this undeniably starts to add up in our life and experience. One of my teachers, Nyoshul Khen Rinpoche, used to say, "When we plant a seed in the ground, we do not see a huge tree right away. But when we see a little shoot emerging from the ground, we should understand that something has sprouted which, in time and with proper care, will grow into a giant tree." Seeing the shoot should encourage us greatly. We must not neglect it, but nurture and protect our little shoot, so that it can grow to its full potential. At some point, if we do not give up, but continue to apply ourselves, all that we do—eating, breathing, walking, sitting, thinking, and so forth—becomes naturally integrated with our practice of Dharma. Mindfulness and altruism become second nature to us, and we don't waste nearly as much time and energy as we once did. We come to have tremendous ease in our mind and body, like a sailboat whose sails are full of wind, gliding swiftly across the water. We accomplish all that we set out to do in the Dharma, and in other areas of our lives, with joy and lightness of heart.

24

BE THE MASTER
OF YOURSELF

The Art of True Joy

Verses 75 and 76 cover the second strength, wangdu jawa, or "be the master of yourself."

75
By all means, then, before I start some work,
That I might have the strength sufficient to the task,
I will recall the teachings upon carefulness
And lightly rise to what is to be done.

76
Just as flaxen threads waft to and fro,
Impelled by every breath of wind,
So all I do will be achieved,
Controlled by movements of a joyful heart.

When we rely on and take care to cultivate these strengths, our body, speech, and mind become agile, fluid, and flexible. Our strength, clarity, and agility gently guide our mind in any direction we wish, just as a faint breeze can easily stir light cotton threads. Thinking of these verses inspires and motivates us. We joyfully familiarize ourselves with confidence and positive pride in our ability and call upon our mindfulness and internal awareness to keep us on track.

At some point, all that we have been working on and aspiring to becomes second nature. There is only joy. Diligence, or joyful exertion, is learning to train our mind, body, and speech to go in the direction we wish them to go. It is diligence that brings all aspirations to fruition, in both the conventional world and on the spiritual path. Diligence is what made all the great masters into who they became. Diligence is what made their practice effortless and natural, and most especially, joyful in applying themselves for the benefit of others. Diligence is not only about how to accomplish something; it is the art of finding true joy in everything we do.

ACKNOWLEDGMENTS

I would like to thank everyone who helped bring this book to fruition. First, I would like to acknowledge Jennifer Shippee, my beloved partner and longtime student, who worked tirelessly on this book with so much love and devotion both to me and to the teachings on the Diligence Chapter. This compilation weaves together many teachings that I have given over the years on *The Way of the Bodhisattva*, and she has extracted the main points of the Diligence Chapter with clarity and great care.

Diligence allows us to progress on the spiritual path. In this book, we focus primarily on the path of the Mahayana Buddhadharma. Alongside that, we also emphasize how the same principles of diligence can be applied to any aspect of our lives, allowing us to accomplish all that we intend whether worldly or spiritual. I would like to thank Shambhala Publications for giving us the opportunity to bring these unique teachings by Shantideva to a larger audience. In particular, Tasha Kimmet's understanding, care, and gentle guidance through all stages of the publishing process have been a great source of encouragement. Thank you to *everyone* at Shambhala Publications who contributed to making this book as good as it could possibly be and especially to Ashley Benning for her precise copyediting, Dianna Able for faithfully shepherding this book through the production stages, and the imaginative design team who brought a fresh face to the Diligence Chapter with their creation of its singular cover.

I would like to acknowledge and thank Ken Kaliher for diligently working with Jennifer on multiple proofreading sessions. His expert support in this and many other projects is greatly appreciated. I also would like to thank Joseph Waxman and Inaba Daisuke for their help with the glossary, and Joseph for offering valuable suggestions for the manuscript.

Lastly, I want to thank all the readers of this book. I hope you may take the points contained here into your hearts and lives and apply yourselves in various and creative ways to improve your discipline and diligence, which in turn will allow more joy and happiness to flourish and unfold.

I personally lack diligence—but at the same time I know what I need to do to make headway in this life and for my future lives to come to reach enlightenment. It is all contained in the pages of this book.

GLOSSARY

Alaya (Skt.) Our mind stream, which forms the ground of our consciousness; the eighth consciousness within the skandhas.

Aloo-tikki An Indian street food snack.

Application bodhichitta Based on aspiration bodhichitta, this is the actual practice of the bodhisattva's path—that of love, compassion, the six paramitas, and so on; necessary for attaining Buddhahood.

Aspiration bodhichitta The wish to attain enlightenment for the benefit of all beings. This aspiration or wish is the starting point of the bodhisattva path.

Bakchak (Tib.) Habitual reactions, the momentum of old habits.

Bakyö (Tib.) Mindfulness.

Bardo (Tib.) Intermediate state; commonly refers to the period between death and the next rebirth.

Basic Vehicle An English translation of Hinayana, comprising the first set of teachings given by the Buddha. It is also known as the Foundational Vehicle because it includes many basic tenets of Buddhism such as refraining from harming others. It differs from the Mahayana or Great Vehicle mainly in its motivation. Followers of the Basic Vehicle aim to attain nirvana for themselves, whereas students of the Mahayana seek liberation for all sentient beings, including themselves.

Bhumi (Skt.) One of the stages of the bodhisattva path.

Bodhicharyavatara (Skt.) Shantideva's guide to the Mahayana path, translated into English as *The Way of the Bodhisattva* or *Introduction to the Bodhisattva's Way of Life*.

Bodhichitta (Skt.) In Mahayana Buddhism, bodhichitta is the mind (*chitta*) that is aimed at awakening (*bodhi*) with wisdom and compassion for the benefit of all sentient beings. We can also call this the mindset of awakening.

Bodhisattva (Skt.) One who has aroused bodhichitta and taken a vow to free all sentient beings from samsara.

Bodhisattvayana (Skt.) The path of bodhisattvas.

Buddhadharma (Skt.) The Buddha's teachings.

Buddha nature The innate potential of buddhahood present in the mind of every living being to awaken to the unconditional peace that all beings possess.

Chandrakirti The seventh-century scholar who wrote *Introduction to the Middle Way* (Skt. *Madhyamakavatara*).

Chörab namjé kyi shérab (Tib.) Wisdom fully discerning phenomena.

Dak ché dzin (Tib.) Self-importance.

Dak mépa (Tib.) Egolessness; selflessness.

Daknyi nyépé lélo (Tib.) The laziness of habituated self-denigration.

Dana (Skt.) Generosity; the first of the six paramitas.

Déwa (Tib.) Bliss, meaning physical and mental well-being and fulfillment.

Dharma (Skt.) The Buddha's teachings. The word also refers to phenomena: "All dharmas are emptiness."

Dharmakaya (Skt.) Literally, "Dharma body." A term of realization indicating the emptiness aspect of Buddhahood; it refers to realization of the absolute nature.

Dhyana (Skt.) Meditation, concentration; the fifth of the sixth paramitas; *samten* (Tib.).

Dorwa (Tib.) Moderation; one of the four allies.

Dradön drédzin gyi tokché (Tib.) Joining the mental image and mental label of any particular thing and forming a clear understanding.

Dudzi (Tib.) Distracting preoccupations.

Dukkha (Skt.) Suffering.

Four allies Four skills to develop in the practice of diligence: aspiration, steadfastness through developing self-confidence, joy, and resting or taking short breaks. In Tibetan, the four allies are möpa, tenpa, gawa, and dorwa.

Four immeasurables Immeasurable love, compassion, joy, and equanimity. Contemplating these four is foundational to developing aspiration bodhichitta, the wish to attain enlightenment for the benefit of all beings.

Gawa (Tib.) Joy; one of the four allies.

Jawa ngenshen gyi lélo (Tib.) Laziness of attachment to mundane activities; the laziness of distracting preoccupations; *jawa* means "activities" and *nyen* means "insignificant."

Jéluk (Tib.) Heavy.

Jéluk gi lélo (Tib.) Heavy with laziness; a yearning for idleness for its own sake.

Jéluk mépa (Tib.) Being free from laziness or obstacles; literally, "without heaviness."

Karma (Skt.) Action; the law of cause and effect.

Kleshas (Skt.) Destructive emotions; the five poisons of attachment, aggression, stupidity (deep mental fog), arrogance, and jealousy.

Ksanti (Skt.) Patience; the third of the six paramitas; *zöpa* (Tib.).

Kshatriya (Skt.) "Warrior clan" or "royalty"; the second highest of the four castes of traditional Indian society.

Lélo (Tib.) Laziness.

Lhur langwa (Tib.) Make an effort; one of the two strengths.

Lojong (Tib.) Mind training.

Mahayana (Skt.) The Great Vehicle, the practice of which goes beyond the goal of individual enlightenment of the Basic Vehicle to have bodhichitta as its essence.

Mara (Skt.) Literally, "demon"—that which creates obstacles to spiritual practice.

Marungpa (Tib.) Unjust.

The Middle Way The Mahayana spiritual practice which avoids the extremes of sensual indulgence or extreme asceticism and follows the Buddha's teachings on ontological issues concerning personal identity and the nature of existence. The Middle Way steers clear of the philosophical extremes of eternalism and nihilism, and instead explores the empty and dependently arising nature of all phenomenon.

Merit. Sönam (Tib.) The positive force accumulated by engaging in virtuous deeds intended to benefit others, especially when bodhichitta is developed in the beginning and the deed is dedicated in that direction in the end.

Möpa (Tib.) Aspiration; self-inspiration; one of the four allies.

Nangtsul (Tib.) The way things appear—how we grasp and assume them to be (as opposed to *nétsul*, the way things are).

Nangwa dra lang (Tib.) All appearances arise as an enemy.

Nashé döngo (Tib.) A human being; "one who can hear and understand, reply and communicate."

Nétsul (Tib.) The way things are (as opposed to *nangtsul*, the way things appear).

Nirvana (Skt.) A nonreversible state of realization of the nature of all things resulting in the liberation from all suffering. This final result of the Buddhist path differs in the Basic Vehicle, Mahayana, and Vajrayana.

Paramita (Skt.) Transcendent perfection. The bodhisattva path has six paramitas that the bodhisattva engages in stages while both in and out of formal meditation practice.

Prajna (Skt.) Supreme knowledge/wisdom; the sixth of the six paramitas; *shérab* (Tib.).

Pungtsok (Tib.) Marshal all your powers; gathering the four allies. *Pung* means "force or power"; *tsok* means "to gather."

Rochik (Tib.) One taste, referring to the empty-luminous nature of all things.

Sakya Pandita (1182–1251) One of the founders of the Sakya lineage and an emanation of the Bodhisattva Manjushri.

Samsara (Skt.) The cycle of painful existence perpetuated by our disturbing emotions and confused reactions; the indefinitely repeated wheel of birth, misery, and death caused by karma.

Sépa (Tib.) Desire.

Shakyas (Skt.) The clan of a small kingdom of Magadha (in modern-day Bihar, India) in the sixth century B.C.E.

Shamatha (Skt.) Calm abiding; *shiné* (Tib.).

Shantideva (685–763) The great Indian sage who composed the *Bodhicharyavatara.*

Shenpa (Tib.) Fixation; grasping; the self-clinging found in the afflictive emotions; attachment to pleasure and aversion to discomfort; an unconscious level of preference for how we want things to be.

Shézhin (Tib.) Vigilant introspection.

Shila (Skt.) Moral discipline; the second of the six paramitas; *tsultrim* (Tib.).

Shravaka (Skt.) Listener; a practitioner of the Basic Vehicle (Skt. *Hinayana*), who seeks to attain personal liberation.

Shravakayana (Skt.) The path of shravakas; the Basic Vehicle.

Shunyata (Skt.) Emptiness; *tongpa nyi* (Tib.).

Skandhas (Skt.) Literally, "aggregates." The combined relative functional existence of body or form, feelings, conceptions, mental formations, and consciousnesses that make up the basis for clinging to the self.

Small self The contracted sense of "self" that is absorbed solely in one's own needs and wants, oblivious to the needs and wants of others.

Sönam (Tib.) Merit, developed by the practice of positive deeds for the benefit of others.

Sutras (Skt.) Teachings of the Basic Vehicle and the Mahayana.

Tabshé (Tib.) Wisdom and skillful means.

Tathagata (Skt.) Literally, "Thus Gone," an epithet for a buddha; *dézhin shékpa* (Tib.).

Tathagatagarbha (Skt.) Enlightened essence, pure potential, or Buddha nature.

Tenpa (Tib.) Steadfastness; one of the four allies.

Three characteristics of realness Traditionally the "three spheres" of self, others, and action. Believing these three to be real and separate is the definition of cognitive obscuration or not seeing the true nature of phenomena as it is.

Three Jewels The Buddha, the Dharma, and the Sangha. Buddhists take refuge in the Three Jewels: Buddha serves as the guide, Dharma serves as the teachings, and Sangha serves as noble companions on the path.

Three wisdoms Hearing, contemplation, and meditation. These are sequential in application. First, we must hear the wisdom of the Buddha, then we need to contemplate what we have heard to clear our doubts, and finally we meditate upon that point as a means to attain genuine realization.

Timuk (Tib.) Deep mental fog (stupidity or ignorance).

Tonglen (Tib.) The practice of sending and taking, which opens us up to what all beings are experiencing.

Tongpa nyi (Tib.) Emptiness; *shunyata* (Skt.).

Tséwa (Tib.) Tenderness and warmth emanating from a loving heart and shared with all sentient beings free from partiality.

Tsöndru (Tib.) Diligence or joyful exertion.

Tsul min yijé (Tib.) Inaccurate perception of the self. (Short for *tsulzhin mayinpé yijé*.)

Tuk-tuk Auto rickshaw commonly used in India and other Asian countries.

Tun (Tib.) Meditation session.

Two strengths Cultivated in the practice of diligence, the two strengths are "make an effort" and "be the master of yourself." In Tibetan, these two are *lhur langwa* and *wangdu jawa*.

Universal self The expanded sense of "self" that understands how all beings are basically the same—we do not want to suffer and instead wish for peace and happiness. This expanded self includes ourselves and all sentient beings.

Vajradhvaja (Skt.) The Vajra Banner sutra.

Virya (Skt.) Diligence or joyful exertion; the fourth of the sixth paramitas; *tsöndru* (Tib.).

Wangdu jawa (Tib.) Be the master of oneself; literally, "Exerting control"; one of the two strengths.

ABOUT THE AUTHOR

A SPIRITUAL LIFE
IN MODERN TIMES

Photograph by Jakob Leschly

Dzigar Kongtrul Rinpoche descends from a pure lineage of the Dzogpa Chenpo Longchen Nyingtik tradition of Tibetan Buddhism. Born into a noble Dharma family in Northern India, he is a son of the third incarnation of the great tertön Chogyur Lingpa, while Rinpoche's first teacher, his mother Tsewang Paldon, was a renowned practitioner, completing thirteen years of retreat before she married.

At the age of nine, Rinpoche was recognized as an incarnation of Jamgon Kongtrul Lodro Thaye by Kyabje Dilgo Khyentse Rinpoche and the 16th Gyalwang Karmapa. Raised in a monastic environment, Rinpoche received extensive training in all aspects of Buddhist doctrine. In particular, he received the teachings of the Nyingma lineage from his root teacher, Kyabje Dilgo Khyentse Rinpoche. Rinpoche also studied extensively under Tulku Urgyen Rinpoche, Nyoshul Khen Rinpoche, and the great scholar Khenpo Rinchen.

In 1989, Rinpoche moved to the United States and began a five-year tenure at Naropa University as the first holder of the World Wisdom Chair. During that time Rinpoche founded Mangala Shri Bhuti, an organization dedicated to establishing a genuine sangha of the Longchen Nyingtik lineage in the West.

Kongtrul Rinpoche's life defines what it means to be a spiritual person in modern times. Whether through his teaching, his passion as an abstract painter (kongtruljigme.com), his steadfast dedication to his lineage and his students, or his joy in solitude, he shows what it means to have an unshakable determination to engage in the spiritual path. Weaving into his ancient spiritual heritage the many threads of our modern culture, Rinpoche is known for his uncompromising integrity, deep conviction in altruism, and insistence that all beings, whatever their background, can awaken to their own enlightened nature.

Rinpoche is the author of several books, including *It's Up to You: The Practice of Self-Reflection on the Buddhist Path*, *Light Comes Through: Buddhist Teachings on Awakening to Our Natural Intelligence*, *Uncommon Happiness: The Path of the Compassionate Warrior*, *The Intelligent Heart: A Guide to the Compassionate Life*, *Training in Tenderness: Buddhist Teachings on Tsewa, The Radical Openness of Heart That Can Change the World*, *Peaceful Heart: The Buddhist Practice of Patience*, *Like a Diamond*, and *Garland of Upadesha*.

If you are interested in finding out more about pursuing the Tibetan Buddhist spiritual path of the Dzogchen Longchen Nyingtik lineage under Rinpoche's guidance, please visit mangalashribhuti.org.